# THE ULTIMATE GUIDE FOR CEOs

## Peter F. Drucker

A manager sets objectives - A manager organizes – A manager motivates and communicates – A manager, by establishing yardsticks, measures – A manager develops people.

Traditionally, we have searched for the miracle worker with the magic wand to turn an ailing organization around. To establish, maintain, and restore a theory, however, does not require a Genghis Khan or a Leonardo da Vinci in the executive suite. What's required is not genius; it is hard work. It is not being clever; it is being conscientious. It is what CEOs are paid for.

FOREWORD BY LIEUTENANT GENERAL (R...

*A*dvantage
BOOKS

# THE ULTIMATE GUIDE FOR CEOS

## AN EXECUTIVE GUIDE TO MANAGING LARGE, COMPLEX, AND LONG-RANGE PROJECTS

## FORREST WAYNE HEARD

**Library of Congress Catalog Number: 2024933734**

| | |
|---|---|
| **Name:** | Heard, Forrest Wayne |
| **Title:** | *The Ultimate Guide For CEOs* |
| | Forrest Wayne Heard |
| | Advantage Books, 2024 |
| **Identifiers:** | ISBN Paperback: 978159757856 |
| | ISBN eBook: 978159758020 |
| | ISBN Hardcover: 9781597557917 |
| **Subjects:** | Self Help – Leadership |
| | Self Help – Success |
| | Business & Money – Management & Leadership |
| | Entrepreneurship |

First Printing: August 2024

24 25 26 27 28 29   10 9 8 7 6 5 4 3 2

# Endorsements

In his new book ***THE ULTIMATE GUIDE FOR CEOs***, Wayne Heard has hit it out of the park. As a professional leadership teacher / Mentor / Executive Coach, I am always on the lookout for strong new resources from which I can illuminate my students with regard to the art and science of leading well. Wayne, whom I have known for 40 plus years brings a lifetime of experience to his project. He began as a young sergeant in the Army, and rose to senior rank serving our Nation with distinction.

Unlike most people with his level of expertise, Wayne does not spend time tooting his own horn. He acknowledges that all his talent came from "standing on the shoulders of Giants", with whom he served and observed in action. The book is filled with examples of superb leaders in action, doing things we can all emulate. He corroborates the validity of his examples with liberal reference to the highest-level leadership gurus in business and academia.

Chapter 7, "Driving Transformation" is of particular note. Rather than a dry and stuffy treatise on transformation or (worse) some lofty but ethereal mumbo jumbo on transformation, Wayne provides a down to earth and completely usable look at a master in action. He follows Major General Sandy Meloy, a former commanding general of the famed 82d Airborne Division, the All Americans, as he initiates and drives transformation in that unit. This is a personal, hands-on technique that any leader can apply, and it works. It requires the leader to get out from behind their desk, and talk to people. "Leadership by Walking Around", is a trope now. Everyone says to do it, but no one seems to know how. Heard's chapter on Meloy's techniques are the quintessential living example of putting that philosophy into action.

The entire book is excellent, and I will be using it as a resource in my own teaching, but the section on Meloy is worth the cost. It really is that useful and that good.

**Dr. Steven P. Bucci, Colonel, US Army (Retired.),** former Deputy Assistant Secretary of Defense

********

**THE ULTIMATE GUIDE FOR CEOs** should be a go-to resource for everyone in a leadership position. Wayne Heard provides management strategies which simplify the complex and give leaders the tools to spend time, money, and energy more effectively than ever before.

This book distinguishes itself from other leadership books by doing away with empty platitudes and self-congratulatory narrative and laying out the real strategies that are employed by top leaders in successful organizations. In his many years of service to our nation as an Army officer, I know Wayne has witnessed the effectiveness of these strategies firsthand, and the strong, specific examples he employs will leave the reader feeling like they have too.

**Lieutenant General William B. Caldwell IV, US Army (Retired),** President of Georgia Military College

********

Wayne Heard, has perfectly captured the essence of Bob Jackson's incredible leadership. COL Jackson's experience, management, and daily example, are his legacy to our Army and our Nation, as those of us fortunate enough to have served with him go on to reflect his teaching, coaching and mentorship. The skills we learned under his training and guidance are more than just military focused - they are lifelong lessons in leadership.

**Lieutenant General Francis "Frank" Wiercinski, US Army (Retired)**

********

Wayne Heard's new book **THE ULTIMATE GUIDE FOR CEOs** is a great must-read for leaders in an organization and would be of interest to anyone wanting their business to succeed. It is a well-written book combining a lifetime of personal and professional experiences in both the military and civilian spectrums. A comprehensive practical resource guide for business owners and corporations alike; filled with anecdotes, and useful pathways and strategies for success. This book may be recommended as one of the clearest handbooks on how transformational leadership can improve the overall functioning of an organization. Highly recommended!

**Jamie G. Herbert, former University Educational Advisor**

From the battlefield to the boardroom, Wayne Heard has written the ultimate guide to organizational effectiveness! If you want to know how U.S. Army Special Forces Officers create order out of chaos, this is for you!

Mission Accomplished, Wayne Heard has written the definitive guide to project organization, management, and success! In this time of over dependence on technology Heard focuses on the #1 resource of any organization… ITS PEOPLE! Leveraging his expertise from years of service as an Army officer and Green Beret, Wayne has a unique perspective on leading and organizing the most complex projects under the most demanding conditions. This is a must read for anyone seeking to organize and lead projects big and small.

**From Mark Shoaff, Master Sergeant, Florida State Patrol, Bureau of Criminal Investigation and Intelligence**

********

*THE ULTIMATE GUIDE FOR CEOs* by Wayne Heard is an extremely useful tool for any decision maker, leader, manager, and/or planner to have in their tool box of references. Highly organized and very well laid out, it can be used as a quick reference guide or an in-depth project analyzer.

Mr. Heard uses credible sources and first-hand experiences to support his ideas and methods. He has taken existing planning techniques and tailored them so that they are useful in any organization whether civilian or military. He also has original thoughts that are insightful, as well.

I strongly recommend this book for anyone who aspires to lead in any field of endeavor, civilian or military. *THE ULTIMATE GUIDE FOR CEOs* is a must have in anyone's personal library.

**Charles W Higbee, Colonel US Army (Retired),** Former Chairman, Department of Academic Affairs, US Army War College; Former Assistant for Planning and Requirements, Office of the Secretary of Defense for Special Operations and Low Intensity Conflict

********

Wayne Heard's book *THE ULTIMATE GUIDE FOR CEOs* is compelling and provides a dynamic approach to problem solving. These principles are applicable to all levels of military command or civilian management. The book is an in-depth study of methods and practices that will improve one's chances of success. It is well researched and full of good examples – "lessons learned have to be discussed and corrected," "failures are failures," "learn to ask the right questions," and "after action reviews start immediately." This book is well written and deserves attention.

**Kief Tackaberry, Colonel US Army (Retired),** Former Director, Army Program (Northrop Grumman Corporation)

********

# Foreword

In my first assignment to a combat unit after graduating from West Point, I served in the 1st Battalion, 19th Infantry "The Rock of Chickamauga", 1st Brigade, 25th Infantry Division, at Schofield Barracks, Hawaii. It was in the 19th Infantry that I encountered a leader who would have a profound impact on me throughout my career—Colonel Robert Louis Jackson.

Colonel Jackson, a central figure in THE ULTIMATE GUIDE FOR CEO's, commanded the 19th Infantry and serves as an exemplar for excellence in execution. I have often said that after serving as a lieutenant under Jackson, everything else came easy.

In Spring of 1981, with the memories of Vietnam receding into history, DESERT STORM nine years in the future, and the "China Threat" not even on our radar, the U.S. Army was solely focused on the Soviet threat in Western Europe. In terms of priorities for equipment and personnel, Hawaii was at the very end of the Army supply chain. While we did train for combat to defend South Korea, our days were not that much different than the pre-WWII lifestyle depicted in the movie, "From Here To Eternity".

All of this changed with the arrival of one remarkable leader who changed many of our lives and careers forever- Lieutenant Colonel Jackson.

"Bob" Jackson hailed from the hills of Tennessee via ROTC at Vanderbilt University. Bob's sole focus was the US Army, leadership of his unit and making sure that we were ready to defend the nation at a moment's notice. Our training exercises increased and became much more realistic. When we returned from training, nobody went home until our equipment was cleaned, repaired and ready to go to war at a moment's notice.

Bob was an expert tactician, a stern, no-nonsense dedicated teacher, and a demanding leader who did not suffer fools lightly. He was both a student and a master of military leadership.

As a black, West Point graduate from New Jersey, with two small children, no two people could have been more different than Bob and me. Our relationship would never have been described as a friendship. That said, our lack of a personal relationship did not stop him from becoming my teacher and mentor. It was Bob who selected me over more senior officers to be his air operations officer. He painstakingly and often painfully drilled into me the fundamental tenets of military planning and leadership. He ensured every leader under his tutelage was engaged in stretch activities.

It was Bob Jackson who routinely placed me in, or secured for me positions of leadership far above my rank, during my time in the 25th Infantry Division. Many years later when I aspired to an assignment with the 82nd Airborne Division, and even though I had no experience in an airborne unit, it was Bob Jackson who vouched for me and helped secure the assignment.

Even though we were never friends, he made it his mission to make me a better soldier and leader so I could make the maximum contribution to his beloved Army. I owe him more than I can say.

The leadership lessons I learned from LTC Bob Jackson served me well during my 41-year military career and remain relevant in my life in the private sector. Wayne has expertly captured the salient points of Jackson's leadership style and management systems within the covers of this book. It is my hope that THE ULTIMATE GUIDE FOR CEO's will pass on those lessons to all who read it.

**Lieutenant General (Retired) Charles Hooper**, US Army. Former Director of Defense Security Cooperation Agency

# Acknowledgements

There are many senior leaders and friends I must acknowledge for their roles in bringing THE ULTIMATE GUIDE FOR CEOs into existence—leaders for providing the exemplars of excellence and friends who reminded me of events and encouraged me to gather this information into one source to help future leaders execute with excellence.

The senior leaders include Generals Frederick Kroesen, Thomas Tackaberry, J.J. Lindsay, James B. Vaught, and Guy S. Meloy. The echelon of leadership with whom I was more closely associated include Colonels Robert L. Jackson, Kief Tackaberry, Darrell Katz, Elliott P. "Bud" Sydnor, Stan Florer, and Tim Waters.

Several of those I call friends rose to the highest levels of leadership within the U.S. Army and Department of Defense and continue to serve the nation in various capacities— leaders like LTG (R) William Caldwell IV, LTG (R) Charles Hooper, and LTG (R) Frank Wiercinski, along with former Deputy Assistant Secretary of the Defense Dr. Steven Bucci.

The information contained in this book describes the activities and values of the leaders who were serving at the highest management levels when I encountered them. The praise for the contents of this book comes primarily from fellow officers who served with these senior leaders. The endorsements refer to the activities of those senior leaders versus my skills in riveting a reader.

My self-imposed mission was to capture the information about those singularly skillful leaders and help the reader understand how the activities of these leaders can be implemented in any organization—be it a public or private, military or civilian, for profit or non-profit.

I must thank two friends who read the earlier drafts of THE ULTIMATE GUIDE FOR CEOs with able pens and critical eyes—Colonel (US Army Retired) Randy Bissell and Ms. Jamie Herbert. They improved this final version more than the reader could ever know. I take full responsibility for the contents, errors in grammar, and final results, but their work greatly increased the readability of this book.

Another friend and mentor, who guided my understanding of comprehensive task analysis, and how to use the results to drive change in multiple United States Government departments and organizations is Michael Dozier. In the world of Personnel Recovery (rescue operations), there are very few people, if any, who have had more impact in the Departments of Defense and Justice as Mr. Dozier.

My final acknowledgement is to the Atlanta business consultant who is regularly referred to within the book. He was a constant source of encouragement for this project. I regularly visited the font of his expertise. He had an immense capacity for pointing me to the writings of, or about, various management gurus and practitioners whose work and quotations could be used to add impact to a point I wanted to make. I refer to him as the Atlanta business consultant; the insightful teacher who taught, If You Can Tie Your Shoes, You Can Learn Physics; the former Army lieutenant who participated in a very effective after-action review / report process in Viet Nam; and the young manager who, when presented with a problem a corporation had wrestled with for a few years suggested, in his first meeting as a member of the management team, "Isn't that long enough to have solved the problem?" This walking encyclopedia of management writing and thought is my brother, Stan Heard.

I hope you enjoy the book as you learn from some of the most accomplished leaders to have served our nation.

# Table of Contents

# Introduction

Developing critical skills for planning and executing long-range, complex, and, even, enduring projects will consistently distinguish you from others as you serve your community, your corporation, or the nation, in positions of greater responsibility. The earlier you develop the critical knowledge, skills, and abilities (KSA) to effectively manage projects, the sooner your upward trajectory to senior executive leadership and the faster your velocity. People respond to managers who execute with excellence.

## Why another Book on Project Management?

You will find most books on the subject of project management, and on-line references are focused on software tools or training-related sites to increase your competence in using software to manage projects. There are few that serve as guides to managing a project—the people engaged in a project—at the executive level. This book describes how a few senior leaders managed multiple projects and developed their leadership teams to execute with excellence.

## For your consideration

How many of you have seen projects start with great fanfare only to witness the energy levels within the team wane, as time passes; projects totally abandoned; or anticipated results scaled back, as managers and senior leaders became distracted or lost confidence? Perhaps the behavior of some members of the project team revealed a lack of real commitment to the project.

One can only imagine how many projects in the public and private sectors are canceled, every year, after valuable resources have been expended in launching them, and valuable time lost in laboring on them. Or, when completed, the product doesn't satisfy the requirement.

## Does this sound familiar?

Have you witnessed the completion date of a project, thought to be vital to your corporation's competitive position, pushed to the right (postponed) several times? Or seen the systematic scaling back of the initial, optimistic, anticipated results of a new product rollout?

### A missed deadline could equal missed opportunities.

Maybe you have personally endured the frustration of serving as a project manager and encountered a lack of zeal from other team members, and you felt you were dragging participants to the finish line.

In this book, you'll learn how you can use the techniques of savvy senior executives to eliminate these frustrating features of running a project.

As you begin this journey of understanding how a few very successful senior executives ensure their initiatives succeed, you are invited to accept a few simple, working definitions and concepts for a shared understanding. These will be introduced in the Preface. Periodically, you'll be introduced to additional resources to increase your understanding and appreciation of the concepts and activities used to manage projects, or drive change at the senior executive level.

### Four Main Objectives in this book

You will learn how to:

- …USE *inclusive brainstorming* techniques to identify the tasks, and increase team member and organizational buy-in, with fewer tasks popping up unexpectedly during the execution.

- …EMBED activities into the plan to manage successful execution.

- …EMPLOY simple leadership activities to maintain high energy levels—the zeal—so commitment remains optimal throughout the project, even for those long-range or enduring projects; and…

- …CAPTURE lessons learned—the good ideas and cautions—so you, and your team, improve your skills for executing the next project.

In addition to the four main objectives, you'll learn how to:

- Establish a professional development (and mentoring) program to increase the project management skills of all members of your team, thereby increasing synergy throughout the organization.

- Employ *cross-training* to give depth to your bench strength, a technique long used by U.S. Army Special Forces teams.

- Broaden your professional development program to develop, or upgrade, the knowledge of the team members to include areas outside of their personal expertise.

- Develop an effective, lessons-learned program (in which the focus is on implementation, with the end game of making lasting improvements in organizational processes beginning immediately).

- Support your senior executive's project, as a project manager (when you aren't the senior executive and project owner).

- Implement a new policy or process, and even change the culture, ensuring the policies and changes are understood and embraced by the entire organization.

- Pierce the *band of inhibitors* to ensure your vision and instructions are understood, and vital feedback reaches you.

- Conduct highly effective meetings as the senior executive, or project lead.

- Make your transition from 'bench chemist' or line supervisor to project manager or senior executive / project owner.

- Drive lasting change in large, complex organizations.

## What this book is not.

This book is not about project management software tools, although you will be introduced to one simple tool. The effectiveness of this tool has been proven in the management of the most complex projects along with the most straightforward routine projects organizations face daily. But the focus of this book is on managing the people involved in the project and executing with excellence. One problem I have found, all too often, is some leaders fall in love with the software, but won't even casually flirt with solid management techniques. Real management doesn't seem to interest them, greatly. They equate a good tool with management.

This book is not based on extensive research, nor is it an academic study. The information you'll find in these pages include a lifetime of observations of effective and successful leaders / managers, and suggestions for implementing these lessons in your work. You'll take a 'right seat ride' shadowing senior leaders who executed well. The techniques are reinforced by the writings of, or about, exemplars of management.

# Preface

# Setting the Conditions for Effective Project Management

"*The After-Action Report starts now!*" With these words, Robert L. Jackson would begin every project—large or small, simple or complex, short-term or long-range. His entreaty to everyone, and his actions throughout the life cycle of each project, established an expectation that his would be a learning organization. Everyone involved would be expected to identify shortcomings and provide recommendations to improve every process and procedure. He expected incremental improvements learned from each undertaking.

Henry Ford. "**It is always possible to do a thing better the second time.**"

By personal demonstration, Jackson revealed the activities managers can employ to develop and maintain excellence in an organization. This leader instilled, into the people of his organization, a consciousness regarding the inter-related disciplines of execution, reflection, and continuous improvement, while creating a few disciples along the way. His technique of managing—at the senior executive level—is worthy of study.

**NOTE**: All military terms and organizations are explained in the glossary.

In these pages, you'll learn habits and disciplines—the tips, techniques, and activities— used by Jackson and other gifted leaders to manage the most complex projects for which your office, division, or corporation is responsible. You'll learn to nurture, within your organization, a culture of excellence in execution.

Aristotle: "**We are what we repeatedly do. Excellence, then, is not an act, but a habit.**"

Although the basis for these tips and techniques is derived primarily from Bob Jackson, not every idea presented for your consideration comes from this one gifted manager. In addition, you'll also witness the work of a relatively short list of executives who showed remarkable abilities in managing large organizations and activities.

## Transformational Management and Inclusive Brainstorming

You will be introduced to a leader who was an exemplar for managing transformation in large complex organizations. Another was innovative in establishing an inclusive brainstorming protocol that can significantly reduce those unwelcomed surprises that often pop-up during a major project—surprises no one on the core team would have foreseen. This inclusive style provides the additional benefit of increasing the level of support for the project, and the process, throughout the organization.

You have probably been involved in a few projects if you are reading this book. You may have seen a project that started out well but ran out of steam; was canceled; or failed to deliver what was expected. In this book, you'll examine the habits of leaders who executed well and prevented subpar results. You'll observe how talented leaders reinforce the positive aspects of human nature, and short-stop a few common human failings that can adversely affect execution of a project. These shortfalls are especially prevalent in those long-term projects that seem to slide down the scale of importance in the minds of those participating, as time passes.

People and activities must be managed to ensure their work is aligned with organizational goals and the projects on which you have responsibility. One sage who ran a tree farm told me, **"Even a hole has to be managed."** If you've ever seen a hole that has been ignored for a month or so, you will have noticed the sides begin to cave in, the bottom fills with sediment. What was a hole becomes, in time, merely a depression.

All management is really managing the activities of people. And, unfortunately, not all employees are as talented or committed as one would like. After all, **"Not all Soldiers are like Uriah."**

## Maintaining Commitment

Inside these pages are examples of managers (project owners) who skillfully ensured the level of commitment and zeal towards supporting long-range projects were maintained at the highest levels throughout execution.

A few senior leaders contributed just one or two ideas to this body of knowledge, but whose insights made a world of difference in the development, and execution, of a comprehensive course of action.

## Habits and Disciplines

The objective of this book is to provide you with a roadmap—a system of habits, disciplines, and activities for developing excellence in execution throughout the organization, be it in the public or private sector. These activities aren't going to be hard to execute or understand. They will be simple strategies you can begin employing immediately. They are easy to do. But as Jim Rohn, the business philosopher, often said, **"What is easy to do is easy NOT to do."**

## Closing an Army Base in Germany and Moving to another City

The main project that serves as the genesis, and leitmotif, of this book is the closing of a U.S. Army base in a small town in Bavaria. It involved moving the entire organization to another city and state, in Germany. In fact, the base commander had responsibility for managing the move of three disparate units that were transplanted to three separate bases in Germany.

This move involved transplanting soldiers and their families, along with moving their personal household goods and corporate headquarters furniture and equipment. The corporate equipment included an extensive array of weapons, night vision devices, and more exotic equipment, along with the transfer of ammunition stockpiles necessary for training. The base closure required a separate plan for returning ownership and control to the government of Germany. The move included building and renovating facilities at the receiving base. Throughout the move, the unit was expected to maintain a high operations tempo.

## The Gulf War – A Major Obstacle to Execution

During the planning and preparation phases, the organization was alerted and executed a short-notice deployment to conduct combat operations in support of OPERATION DESERT STORM, the first Gulf War. Combat was followed by a mission to support several hundred thousand refugees in an austere environment—OPERATION PROVIDE COMFORT. The unit was away from home station and families from January until June of that year, and the move—the execution phase—began immediately upon its return to Germany. The deadline to hand over the keys to the base to the German government had been established long before the deployment. This date had become nonnegotiable.

The closing of a military base and the move to an unfamiliar city and state within Germany is not unlike moving a corporate production facility from one state to another. Except in the States, you probably won't have to worry about getting shot at during your planning and execution phases. The process for developing a comprehensive plan for the corporation certainly parallels the work these planners undertook.

## The Task

Imagine you've been given the unenviable task of closing your corporation's plant and moving operations from a town where it has been located for the past 50 years. Corporate headquarters has challenged your management team to maintain the same level of output from the production line.

## Week One

As the move unfolds, equipment and the necessary parts supporting each step in the production process are moved—along with the employees who operate that equipment. The production line must be reestablished and returned to action within three weeks of departing.

## Weeks Two - Four

Week number one is devoted to packing out the employees' homes and disassembling the production equipment and loading it for shipment. Just-in-time deliveries for each step in the production must diminish, then stop for the departure location, and begin arriving in greater quantities at the other location.

Week two is focused on settling the uprooted families in their new homes. A third week is allowed for setting up the production line. At the end of week number four, the CEO expects you to be up and running and meeting normal production goals.

## Competing Activities

In addition, your staff, managers, and first-line supervisors will be required to receive, in-process, and train new hires, while providing support for those employees and families who choose not to make the move. A complementary plan for moving the administrative support personnel and activities is required to support both departure location and the new site, while personnel from human resources also settle into homes in an unfamiliar city.

## Complementary Values

Planning a move with the least interruption to family life, while maintaining team (production line) integrity and pursuing an aggressive production schedule, was the challenge. The move was described as a series of collapsing balloons, balloons that collapsed at the departure end, and reappeared and re-inflated, at the far end. Balloons being the teams, management activities, equipment and supplies; and training.

## Insights into Developing the Plan

There was a structured process for developing the initial plan. However, additional activities were incorporated into the plan based on ideas and techniques the team members had witnessed in past projects and previous assignments.

Insights from other members of your organization can add to the comprehensive list of tips, techniques, and procedures (TTP) you'll be able to employ as an executive, the individual tasked with the day-to-day oversight of a project, or the team reporting to the executive on the status of the activities supporting the project.

You'll discover that many of the effective disciplines, activities, and mindsets of those you encounter in this book are reflected in the writings of management theorists and observers, e.g. Deming, Drucker, Collins, Goldratt, and Peters, and writings by and about effective practitioners—Bossidy, Gerstner, and Welch.

## Surprising Shortfall

Surprisingly, otherwise talented managers are often unaware of these simple techniques that put into practice the theories they were, undoubtedly, introduced to in their academic endeavors and certifications.

These good, competent managers are often diligent, educated, intelligent, personable, and seemingly in possession of all the knowledge necessary for managing projects. These managers aren't considered problem managers, who go about destroying the morale of an organization. They are roll-up-their-sleeves leaders. Personality and supervisory skills aren't the issues.

Perhaps, these young managers weren't exposed in their careers to someone possessing the management skills to execute at such a distinctly higher level like the ones you'll get to know in this book. Quite possibly, they weren't seasoned enough to have recognized that singular extraordinary manager when in the presence of one and neglected to observe the key techniques the manager used. *"When the student is ready, the teacher will appear."*

There is a legend about the nightingale that says the bird won't sing (can't sing) until it's heard another nightingale sing. If one were to take a young nightingale away to a distant location where there are no nightingales, it would never learn to sing. Possibly, it's the same in management. Maybe you must serve with one of the truly gifted managers to learn the song.

To help in understanding the concepts presented over these pages, it will prove helpful to explain the definitions of terms and concepts as they are used here.

### Management and Leadership

First: how do you describe management? There is literature, and significant debate, suggesting there is a divide between managers and leaders with each engaging in distinct activities. This book does not subscribe to that concept. The insights and activities around which this book is organized will include the four functions of management that textbooks frequently use: plan, organize, lead, control. There will be no division between managers and leaders. A manager must be competent in all four functions. Leading is a subset of managing. (In discussing the activities of a leader, a manager, a project owner, or an executive the titles will be used interchangeably…for literary purposes, depending on the primary activities under consideration.)

In the introduction to the revised edition of Management, by Peter F. Drucker, Jim Collins writes: **"As Peter Drucker shows right here, in these pages, the very best leaders are first and foremost effective managers. Those who seek to lead but fail to manage will become either irrelevant or dangerous, not only to their organizations, but to society."**

W. Edwards Deming says, **"To manage one must lead. To lead, one must understand the work that he and his people are responsible for."**

You may have heard someone remark that Joe is a great manager, but not much of a leader. Or Beth is a great leader but can't plan or oversee projects, effectively. A manager who can't lead, or a leader who can't plan or organize, can't be considered among the great managers or great leaders. A golfer who can't putt is not a great golfer. And one certainly can't say, "He's a great pilot but just has trouble taking off and landing". To earn a place in the great category, you must be competent in all four functions of management.

Within the functions of management, this will be the working definition of leadership: **The actions you take, and the environment you create for those with whom you work, to accomplish worthwhile goals and objectives with your family, community, work, nation, and the world.**

## Project

Second, what is a project? Consider any activity that involves the coordinated work of more than one person a project. If it only requires one person to do it, it is an activity, a task.

A project might be the implementation of a new policy or process; the relocation of a production facility; or rolling out the new marketing plan. A project might involve changing the culture of an entire organization. (Changing a culture or improving the quality of output is one of the most exciting ventures reported in these pages. The leader changed the organization with aplomb and authority, using simple techniques that any leader can employ.)

## Responsibility

Third, who is responsible? In this work, you should come to understand effective managers take personal responsibility for every project their office, division, or organization has undertaken.

As Drucker is quoted as saying, "**Productivity is not the responsibility of the worker, but of the manager.**"

## Project Owner

Unlike a person christening a ship, the astute executive doesn't see his or her job finished after launching the project. As the senior person in the organization, they see themselves as the **project owner** of every project, and they ensure, through word and deed, everyone involved appreciates that personal commitment.

Embracing personal responsibility does not suggest great project owners are micromanagers. None of the effective leaders about whom you'll read in this work fell into that category. In fact, just the opposite was true. They delegated well; mentored effectively; ensured actions met with their high standards by disciplining themselves to follow up routinely; and ultimately achieved their deadlines, and objectives. Some of those deadlines were imposed from outside of the organization and some were generated from within.

## Project Manager

The project manager (PM) administers the tools used by the organization and keeps everyone on track with requirements. A key insight: When it is widely understood the senior executive considers himself, or herself, the project owner, project manager work can be significantly less frustrating.

## Human Behavior

In the organization that executes well, the project owner takes advantage of the competitive aspect of human behavior. Employees don't want to fail their bosses, nor do they want to look bad in front of others, especially the boss. In *The Economist* article about The Hawthorne Effect, Nov 3rd, 2008, there is mention of the human instinct of association. It is described as the desire to stand well with one's fellows.

When the executive shows up for every status meeting and shows interest, the direct reports will be actively engaged in the execution.

Conversely, in those organizations in which the senior executives no longer involve themselves after the project has been assigned, one can often encounter the frustrated project manager. When the boss quits showing interest in the project, many others will often follow suit. If the senior manager habitually sends a deputy, other department leaders will begin sending deputies.

There will be more definitions later, but these should suffice to lead you into Chapter 1.

- Management includes all four functions plan, organize, lead, and control.

- The senior leader is the project owner and takes responsibility for all aspects of the project—executed to standard, completed on time, and supported throughout the organization and the life cycle of the project.

- The project manager administers the project.

Again, for literary impact, you will see the terms office, directorate, division, corporation, or business used when describing the structure in which the project management team works.

One word about the concept of responsibility: Organizations possessing a high level, or those desiring a high level of executability, there is (and must be) a commensurate level of acceptance of total responsibility for everything the organization does (accomplishes) or doesn't do. This can be one of the toughest values to inculcate, and most difficult to embrace by young managers.

## Responsibility versus Fault

When something goes amiss on the production line because a rank-and-file employee failed to throw a switch or tighten a bolt, the responsibility falls on whom? If the restrooms or break rooms aren't tidy, how is the manager held responsible? The concept of responsibility can be hard for the young member of the management team to accept. Everything that goes on, in his or her slice of the organization, is his or her responsibility, including the cleanliness of the restrooms, and break rooms.

Responsibility doesn't indicate fault. But, without accepting (internally) that "everything that happens within my section is MY responsibility", it is difficult to identify the issues and install the solutions. "What actions can I take to ensure this always happens (the good things) or never happens (the bad things)?" (Hopefully, this studied reflection occurs before an incident.)

Responsibility is a key concept you will have to understand to appreciate this work and to develop a high-reliability organization.

## Self-Help and Management Books

You may have enjoyed the experience of reading other self-help, or management books that resulted in your saying routinely, "Hmm, that idea makes sense" or "Yes. I've seen that work." You may have found yourself quietly nodding in agreement with an idea or concept. Hopefully, this book will generate similar responses from you.

As you review these illustrations of excellence in action, you should be able to see how a technique could work, and more importantly how it can work for you. This book is effective if referred to routinely. Refer to it as you manage projects, serve on project teams, report to senior leaders on the status of projects, or as you serve as the senior executive leading your organization towards excellence in execution.

In their book *Execution: The Discipline of Getting Things Done,* Larry Bossidy and Ram Charan describe the ability to execute as the essence of real leadership.

## Organization of the Book

**Part I** will focus on understanding the process at the macro level. Analyzing all aspects of a project; developing a plan of action, managing the execution, and capturing the lessons for improving your skills for the next undertaking. Although you may find the lead chapters a bit long, you'll soon discover the chapters towards the end of the book tend to be shorter.

**Chapter 1 - Getting Started** summarizes the activities inherent in executing a plan, from receiving and analyzing the project through completion and review for improvement. As Deming explained, **"If you can't describe your process, you don't have one**." Chapter 1 describes the process. In this chapter, you'll have an opportunity to organize your thoughts and create bins for the information presented in later chapters. Like a roll-top desk, the pigeonholes will allow for the information to be archived for easy retrieval.

**In Chapter 2 -Task analysis and Planning**, you'll discover (or be reminded of) how to develop a robust, comprehensive plan using *structured task analysis* and *inclusive brainstorming*. In keeping with the *leitmotif* of closing the production facility (the Army base) and moving to another state, you'll see how the project owner included, not just the core planners, but spouses with their concerns; families with special needs children, along with parents who used German medical facilities in the local area; structural engineers who certify safety of buildings, into which the organizations would move; and even members of the civilian communities who were going to be on the losing end of the closing plus those on the gaining end of the move; etc.

Dale Carnegie. **"People support a world they helped create."**

Another insight reported in The Economist article on the Hawthorne Effect was the conclusion by the research team that one factor in increased productivity was the "opportunity to discuss changes before they took place."

The process you'll see described will help maximize synergy and create an unsurpassed level of buy-in, throughout the organization, in the process and the plan.

The leader you'll be introduced to in Chapter 7 - Driving Transformation, used a similar technique to adjust mindsets, change a culture, and install lasting changes in an organization.

Even if one were to develop the most comprehensive plan ever recorded, this alone will not guarantee success. Managers must actively ensure all the activities are executed on time and to standard.

**Chapter 3 - Managing the Execution** will reveal how to ensure plans are executed, through the management activities of the project owner. If you have ever sat through an ineffective meeting, or heard the lament, "meetings are a waste of time", you'll enjoy this chapter. It dissects and digests meeting discipline, the protocols that maximize the effectiveness of people coming together to report the status to the project owner.

Drucker: **"Plans are only good intentions unless they immediately degenerate into hard work."**

**"A decision is a commitment to action."**

**"No decision has, in fact, been made until carrying it out has become somebody's work assignment and responsibility - and with a deadline. Until then, it's still only a hope."**

## Discipline

Unfortunately, this word is often perceived in a negative manner. For the purposes here, don't think of a harsh disciplinarian model, where punishments are a method used for control and correction.

In the context of developing excellence in an organization, the term 'discipline' refers to the habits individuals and organizations adopt in order to execute well. It's a discipline of embracing worthwhile values. It's akin to the discipline of daily practice world-class musicians demand of themselves.

Jim Collins, in his book *Good to Great*, includes a thoughtful description of the value, and its importance, in the chapter A Culture of Discipline.

Collins: "**A culture of <u>discipline</u> is not a principle of business; it is a principle of greatness.**" "**Greatness is not a function of circumstance. Greatness, it turns out, is largely a matter of conscious choice, and <u>discipline</u>.**"

## <u>Software Tools</u>

Although this book is not about software tools, there is a powerful, yet simple, tool that can be (and has been) used for the most complex and long-range projects. It's a tool that can be introduced and understood quickly. It is most useful to the project owner in managing the execution of multiple projects, simultaneously, with one meeting attended by all project leads.

If your organization uses a software tool (and you most certainly do), don't discard it. But managing at the senior executive level, and for those who report progress to a senior executive, may require a different tool of choice. By using the technique described in this chapter, the information a senior executive requires to manage a project is simply and cleanly displayed. It allows the senior executive to absorb the vital information quickly and manage multiple projects, effectively. (The key concept here is 'effectively'.)

The most endearing qualities of the tool are it can be used to manage the smallest project—projects like company picnics—or the most complex, like the support and defense of four large refugee camps straddling the international border of two countries (Turkey and Iraq) along with the feeding and housing of, and providing medical treatment to, hundreds of thousands of refugees, in remote, snow-covered, mountainous locations.

An important benefit of using the same task analysis process and management tool for every project, regardless of size and complexity, is you become faster and better at examining a task, developing comprehensive plans, and managing the execution.

## <u>Identifying Shortfalls Early</u>

In Chapter 3, you will be introduced to a few activities that reveal shortfalls early, allowing quick responses by management and installation of solutions that all but guarantee successful execution. You'll see how senior leaders ensure the energy levels are maintained throughout the project, as well as eliminating the tendency for team members to fall into the term-paper mentality, and provide for the collection of lessons learned (tips, cautions, and ideas) throughout the life cycle of the project.

## Skill versus Cutting-Edge Technology

A word about tools versus education, training, knowledge, skills, and abilities:

Imagine you have inherited the craft shop machines and material from your favorite uncle or aunt. You fall in love with the jigs, the wood, the saws, and the stained glass. Every tool and device for creating beautiful furniture, or stained glass is now at your fingertips. You envision yourself crafting fine furniture, or tightly-fitted stained glass side panels for your front door.

In the excitement of your good fortune, you attend a major home show at the local convention center. As you tour the various booths, you come upon one in which a master craftsman constructs fine furniture using only tools that were available in the 19th Century.

Imagine the results, if you were to compete against this master craftsman armed with tools from the 19th Century, while you had the latest 21st Century tools at your disposal, but you had no education, training, or experience. Who do you think would turn out the tightest dovetail joints? To take the analogy further, do you think the quality would suffer if the master craftsman used the 21st Century tools?

The reason I use this illustration is that routinely newspapers report of a poorly-performing government department, administration, or agency attempting to solve management issues by investing in more expensive, state-of-the-art software. This, alone, rarely (if ever) solves the problem.

Organizations that are well-run with older tools can certainly outperform poorly run organizations that possess the latest tools, if those poorly-managed organizations don't upgrade other aspects of management that lead to excellence.

NOTE: This book is not advocating a return to the 3X5 index cards for management. It is proposing that project management tools are most effectively employed by those who are already skillful managers, regardless of the tool selected by their corporations or organizations.

This phenomenon of attempting to use a purchase to solve a lack of expertise in managing is not limited to software solutions. Corporations can fall prey to the temptation in hardware, as well.

Suppose a poorly-managed organization wants to increase productivity and purchases a machine that has a rated capacity of 4 times the current output of 'x' widgets per day. The old machine's rated capacity was actually 2 times but the management team never realized that level of production. The new machine can become a labor-saving device for the employee who uses it, without any increase in productive results to the organization. The employee may discover he or she can produce the same number of widgets every day, with less effort. If the corporation experiences the same daily results, the machine has merely become an additional cost.

**Chapter 4 - The Learning Organization** will focus on constantly improving the organization - the people and processes - by examining the centerpiece of improvement, the after-action report, along with daily improvement. You will see how to collect lessons learned, ensure the information is spread across the organization, and infuse the improvement throughout the organization's DNA—processes and culture.

You'll be encouraged to adopt a mindset of lessons learned not as a noun (LESSONS learned) but as a verb (lessons LEARNED and applied).

You'll see how to eliminate a prevalence to allow lessons to be observed but ultimately forgotten, as team members are promoted, move to different jobs within the corporation, or even leave the organization.

Establishing an expectation of an after-action review and a requirement to constantly look for improvements will energize the reticular activating system, so opportunities and necessary adjustments reveal themselves.

You will see how to ensure incremental improvements are captured and installed, changing the way you do business, immediately.

At the end of this chapter, you'll be introduced to D-day planning. This is not about the June 6, 1944 invasion to liberate Europe, but the conversion of your completed project into a D-day tool to inform your next planning session and project.

## Part II

Chapters in Part II will introduce or expand on the information that supports professional development of your organization (large or small). You'll be introduced to activities useful in developing the skills of the individual members in your office in managing projects, and other core skills necessary to succeed in the organization. These activities will facilitate developing and maintaining excellence throughout the corporation.

**Chapter 5 - Improving Self, Others, and Processes** will be devoted to helping you create, launch, and manage a professional development program. You'll be encouraged to adopt a paradigm shift regarding mentoring. Instead of taking the common, narrow approach of a manager mentoring one, or at most only a handful of direct reports, or a senior executive plucking some rising talent from junior management, you'll be introduced to Bob Jackson's effective group mentoring program. His is a program any leader can implement, right now! You'll learn a few best practices that can be employed, immediately, across an organization to increase the quality of execution in your core competencies and ancillary activities.

**Chapter 6 - Husbanding the Resources, Taking Care of Capital Assets** will expand on the professional development concept to include training your team to operate and maintain every piece of equipment they may reasonably be called upon to employ, or on which they supervise employees.

Jackson: **"Maintenance is a command responsibility."**

Jackson would routinely remind his management team they must '**husband the resources**'. "The parents have a right to expect we take care of their sons and daughters while they are with us. And the taxpayers have a right to expect we'll take care of the equipment they provide. We'll operate it safely, maintain it, and get the longest use of it before it wears out and has to be replaced." Another one of his pithy remarks was, **"The training isn't over until the equipment is ready to go to war again."**

**Chapter 7 - Transformational Leadership**; Driving Change will introduce a few ideas on transforming large, complex organizations as demonstrated by one of its most successful practitioners—Guy S. Meloy. You'll follow along with him as he drives change and steers a complete turnaround of a very large organization, within a very few months. The process (a few simple activities he initiated) began almost immediately, but the culture of execution and excellence was firmly in place within six months and never regressed during his time as the senior executive. You'll see how the acceleration of change can be increased exponentially with a few informed actions.

**Chapter 8 - Delegation** will take on the task of working through others, with the purpose of developing them and allowing you to manage more activities and larger organizations. Two key points must be stressed about the talented leaders described in this book, regarding their management styles. None were micromanagers but all were heavily invested in, and took personal responsibility for, outcomes.

These executives moved about their organizations constantly checking on people, processes, products, and systems to ensure guidance was understood and implemented, to their standards.

As Gerstner remarked, "**...you cannot run a successful enterprise from behind a desk.**"

Some may suggest this reflects having no confidence in subordinates. Hopefully, you'll not accept that position after reading the chapter.

Drucker: "**Effective decision makers know this and follow a rule, which the military developed long ago. The commander who makes a decision does not rely on reports to see how it is being carried out. Instead, the commander goes out and looks for him or herself.**"

"**Not that he distrusts the subordinate; he has learned from experience to distrust communications.**"

These talented, and dedicated leaders had mindsets and used engagement opportunities to ensure their subordinates succeeded, not as a method of 'gotchas'.

You'll learn why you should delegate; how to delegate; the insurance policy you establish, and the premiums you must pay, as the manager, when delegating.

## Chapter 9 - Long Range Planning

Jackson's leadership team participated in an offsite to establish the plan for the upcoming 24 months. He thoroughly understood organizations, professional development, maintenance management, human behavior, and the practice in which all systems of an organization should be brought together. This is done to ensure goals are met and people (employees and families) are cared for, both professionally and personally. The level of planning and scheduling was comprehensive.

The process of developing the plan was even more instructive than the final plan. The calendar, developed by the subordinate leaders—his direct reports—was comprehensive but allowed plenty of room for flexibility.

**Chapter 10 - Communications** will examine performance management (one-on-one conversations) and corporate communications.

Within a few days of beginning work under Jackson, you were asked to develop a list of objectives and goals you wanted to achieve over the next 12 months. He would discuss each and might ask you to adjust your list based on his personal guidance. He revisited this list with you, monthly, and he talked with you, daily. His willingness to, and discipline in, setting aside time on his very busy calendar to individually counsel with his direct reports, underscored his commitment to developing leaders.

He provided candid feedback and helpful guidance at each of these meetings. One always knew where one stood. He identified improvement opportunities, and organizational strengths. Conducting routine communication also created a strong bond, and comfort level in asking questions and seeking advice. There were countless other ways Jackson stimulated one's performance levels, and energized his team. One really had to "up their game" to compete in Jackson's world.

A Jackson alumnus (Charles Hooper) who went on to serve the nation as a lieutenant general (3 - star) told me, **"After serving as a lieutenant under Jackson, everything else came easy."**

Jackson believed his primary job as a manager—the organization's senior executive—was to develop his leadership team to the degree that each would be successful at increasingly higher levels within the Department of Defense. He created a leadership engine, to borrow a phrase from Professor Tichy.

In this chapter, you'll learn how to help your subordinate leaders develop their annual game plans and increase their proficiencies in every area of the business, thereby increasing their value to the organization.

You'll find a suggestion for shortstopping a potential shortfall or failure in organizations. This method stands in sharp contrast to many management systems that look rearward. Ineffective management systems can often be described as bowling with black curtains strung across the lanes so the bowlers (employees) cannot see where their balls are striking the pins or how many pins are falling. Occasionally, a manager peeks through the curtains and gives them a few clues to their, and the organization's performance...last month.

Deming: "**Managing by results - like looking in the rear-view mirror.**"

Face-to-face communications are important in large organizations, especially those with branch offices spread across the country or across continents. The lack of effective mass communications can lead to uncertainty and can have a powerful, negative impact on the organization.

A lack of consistent, sustained, routine communications by leaders to their teams, and to the whole organization, allows for misinterpretation or confusion among subordinate managers, and the rank and file. Harmful rumors can begin to fill the void.

Those personnel not in the immediate vicinity of the corporate headquarters may never hear the senior executive's commitment to a corporate value. When the climate survey results report field employees aren't confident the executives are committed to an ethical environment, the managers are shocked by the news because they remember discussing it often...in the boardroom.

You may have been in organizations in which corporate headquarters personnel only called when they needed information from you or when they were 'adding to your workload'. This is not due to evil intent. It's just the normal way people go about their workdays. Most are so wrapped up in doing the work in front of them, they don't consider pushing information out and communicating with their distant team members routinely when no actions are required of them.

You'll see how some leaders bypass the band of inhibitors Deming warned against and maintain an open flow of two-way communications. Gerstner certainly understood how to get the word out and down, while staying on top of concerns of employees when he led IBM.

**Chapter 11 - Mission, Vision, and Intent** will summarize the main categories of action to analyze a mission, develop a plan, manage the execution, and learn from a project.

## Part III

There is only one chapter in Part III. In Chapter 12 - Stray **Voltage,** you will find short vignettes that would not fit neatly in chapters 1 through 11.

### Out-of-the-Box Thinking

There will be a tip-of-the-hat to a talented out-of-the-box thinker - Tim Waters - who will demonstrate how to ask questions that produce solutions to issues you face. This was in contrast to the very committed subject matter experts (SMEs) asking unconsciously biased questions that drove unsupportable responses. His technique was similar to the 5 Why method.

The outcome influenced by this creative thinker led to a radically different solution than the several courses of action suggested by the SMEs. In this case, their recommendations would have resulted in an unsupportable and ultimately unsuccessful course of action. Waters looked at the issue with fresh eyes, and a creative mindset.

### Addressing Cold Call Interruptions and Gathering Good Ideas

You'll be introduced to a technique developed for the corporate world to eliminate a common problem experienced by businesses—interruptions of work by sales professionals cold-calling on the company.

You, of course, don't want your management team interrupted during the day, and you don't want your own carefully laid out plan for the day disrupted by sales calls. Nor do you want to discover your competition has adopted a product or program that has accelerated sales or increased employee satisfaction and discover the product representative was shut out by your gatekeeper. You most certainly want to know if there are tools or ideas coming into the market that can increase your competitive edge.

One of the sales professionals out on the street, making those cold calls, trying diligently to get an audience with you, could have provided the solution to a problem with which you are grappling.

The question is: How does your organization ensure all the innovative ideas or potential partners are systematically evaluated, before being adopted or dismissed, while eliminating the plague of cold-call interruptions?

**If you have a problem, develop a process.**

### Taking Over a Project Mid-Stream

Along with miscellaneous good ideas for managers, you'll investigate a few situations faced by you or team like: taking over a project mid-stream; or just before rollout of a new product receiving extra support by untrained help; using knowledge workers; etc.

### Tri-Focal Vision

You'll gain insight into tri-focal vision for planning and problem solving in which you develop solutions at three levels. These levels include: transactional solutions to provide the immediate solution to a problem; integrated, supplementary, and complementary solutions to install for midterm solutions; and foundational solutions that ensure the solution is ingrained in the normal education and training programs of new-hires.

### Management Missteps

We'll touch lightly on a few snares, stumbling blocks, and trip wires to avoid, like snapshot or popcorn management.

### Eliminating Your Mental Roadblocks

Bonus: You'll learn a few insights from a business consultant providing an excellent personal development class to high school seniors en route to college entitled, **"If You Can Tie Your Shoes, You Can Learn Physics"**.

Along the way, sources that are worthy of review will be identified for your further study. These sources will aid you in increasing your skills in managing self, others, or processes.

There is a glossary to help you understand and remember unfamiliar terms you may discover in this book. Quotations contained in this book are also catalogued in the back of the book for your quick reference.

While reading this book, consider taking notes in the margins or keep a record of possible ideas for improving your organization, your own skill set in managing, or your effectiveness in reporting to the senior executive.

*Forrest Wayne Heard*

# Part I

The opening chapters describe:

- The process

- Setting the conditions for success

- Implementing the process

- Gaining and maintaining commitment

- Executing

- Learning from every event

Part I focuses on understanding the process at the macro level, analyzing the task or project, developing a plan of action, managing the execution, and capturing the lessons learned.

# Chapter 1

# Getting Started: The Process

Developing the critical skills necessary for planning and executing multiple, long-range, and complex projects will consistently distinguish you from those who struggle to execute even one project well.

Management expert, Edwards Deming, promulgated the idea **if you could not explain your process, you don't have one**. The quotation, **"If you can't explain it simply, you don't understand it well enough,"** is attributed to Albert Einstein.

This chapter is an introduction to the key processes of developing and executing a plan. Included are a few tips for ensuring the plan is executed well.

Whether nonprofit, for profit, or government office, organizations need leaders who can execute effectively. The more activities you can effectively manage, the greater the likelihood of your success in the organization.

Perhaps you have moved from line supervisor to management, or you've been elevated to senior management. Maybe you showed great skill in managing one project or several, as a project manager. As the adage goes, **'what got you there, won't keep you there'**.

On the other hand, maybe you are already serving in a senior management position, and you aren't pleased with the execution of those projects that fall within your realm of responsibility.

Because emergencies seem to surprise and disrupt your teams regularly, you suspect planning and forecasting are not up to par.

Possibly, you are the senior executive of the organization and you want to install some changes in the organization as a result of a strategic planning session. Maybe you've uncovered behaviors that are in direct conflict with the company values. How do you manage the project, or the initiative to drive change?

After the Bay of Pigs invasion failure in 1961, President John F. Kennedy consulted with former President Dwight D. Eisenhower. One might suspect Ike, the former general and architect of the D-day invasion of occupied France in World War II, would have provided advice on the tactical aspects of an amphibious invasion. Instead, the general asked the young president about his decision-making process.

A critical examination of the discussions leading up to the invasion, and the process changes President Kennedy made after meeting with Ike, can be found in The Art of Critical Decision Making, a course taught by Professor Michael A. Roberto for the Great Courses Corporation.

You, as the senior executive, might also find focusing initially on the process your team uses in developing a plan will pay huge dividends.

## Analyzing the Task

Most types of organizations—commercial, nonprofit, or government—have a structured process for analyzing a task or project. A SWOT analysis in which the strengths, weaknesses, opportunities and threats are investigated might be the most appropriate process for your organization or the project you are undertaking.

The Department of Defense often uses a DOTMLPF-P analysis to determine the changes that will need to occur to adopt a new program or weapons system. The DOTMLPF-P mnemonic refers to doctrine, organization, training, materiel, leadership and education, personnel, facilities, and policies.

Conducting systematic analysis provides the planners with a more robust view from multiple perspectives. By not skipping this critical step, the plan is less likely to encounter unforeseen pitfalls during execution.

## Developing the Plan

With the facts and assumptions laid bare through analysis, your team can develop action steps, when executed on time, should lead to project success.

Identifying the action steps is only one step in developing the plan. You must sequence the steps in a logical order. With sequencing you'll want to highlight the connections among individual tasks. You may find task #123 must be completed before task #40 can begin. As a result, reshuffling the sequence may occur several times.

Establishing a timeline and plotting key dates on it can prove helpful. Identifying the date on which the project must be complete is the most important point on the timeline. You may find working in reverse, from the required completion date to the present, can assist the team in organizing the key activities.

You may want to organize the tasks into 'bins' that support a particular aspect of the project. Identifying the key tasks among the many tasks is also important. These key tasks might inform you in describing the bins.

As you come to agreement with the tasks, how they are interconnected and when they must be completed, you have built the greater portion of your plan. If working with a small team, your next step could be identifying who is responsible for each task. If working in a bureaucracy (government, nonprofit, commercial), established roles and functions within the organization will normally dictate who (or which division, directorate, or office) will have the responsibility for certain lines of effort.

With those elements: the individual tasks, the dates each task must be completed, the office responsible for the task, and the interconnections, you have the essence of the plan. But as Larry Bossidy pointed out in EXECUTION, THE DISCIPLINE OF GETTING THINGS DONE, the most important work now begins.

## Executing the Plan

As Peter Drucker explained, plans are nothing until people roll up their sleeves and get to work. A direct quote by Drucker states, **"Plans are only good intentions unless they immediately degenerate into hard work."** As the executive, you can ensure your projects and plans stay on track by including in every plan, management (oversight) meetings at which the project managers keep you updated on the status of the activities. Schedule the meetings as an integral part of each plan. Establish the expectation those responsible for each task will update you, and the team, on the status of tasks assigned to them.

If you establish the completion dates for the week's activities on the day prior to your meetings—the in-progress reviews—you'll disarm those who may attend meetings without having completed their work. The excuse, "it will be finished by the end of the day" will no longer be valid. (If your meeting is held on Friday, then the completion date should be no later than close of business on Thursday).

Keep in mind, the meetings are held for your benefit and that of the team. In preparing for these meetings, you should review all the tasks that should have been completed since the previous in-progress review (IPR) and study those tasks that should happen before the next IPR. This allows you to identify and discuss those tasks that might need more attention. (It will also signal to your team you are on top of the project and you expect the same from them).

Cautionary note: The IPR is not a meeting to hold conversations about miscellaneous issues unless <u>you</u> are bringing the issues forward. This meeting is a forum at which you are updated. This meeting is for <u>you</u> to ask questions. Any shortfalls that the team is experiencing should have already been reported to the project manager before the meeting so that a plan can be developed to shortstop that failure. Discovering a task is not complete or won't be completed on time should not happen at your meeting.

Increasing the effectiveness of your meetings is a subject covered in Chapter 3 in Meeting Discipline.

## Mitigating Term Paper Mentality

To encourage team members to look forward, review and execute the tasks early and often, a leader must dissuade team members from offering common excuses for the task not being complete.

If a task isn't completed by the no-later-than time (NLT), you can explain that the team (and the organization) is counting on everyone to complete their tasks on time.

If a task has surprised the responsible party by requiring more time to complete than expected, you should use the start date of the project and the due date to compute the elapsed time. Don't accept it couldn't be completed in the week you are currently in. Ensure the team members understand you see the time allowed to complete a task by the total elapsed time since the project began (when appropriate). This will signal to the team (or division heads) you see execution of this project in a different way than they may have seen it.

## Managing Multiple Projects

One particularly effective way to manage multiple projects is to ensure all your project managers, or office heads, use the same format when providing your IPRs. By requiring every project or action reported to you using the same format, the projects can be blended into one management product (display tool). By viewing information in the same format, you can more quickly absorb and identify the key elements of information. Establishing the format that works best for you allows you to more easily identify situations that need your attention.

In addition, with all elements of your organization providing the information in the same format, you can have the information sorted and presented in multiple ways. You can look at all projects; all activities by a particular office; all activities due this week; etc.

If you sense (or determine) a problem area, you can extract one project from the others to focus your attention on a "deep dive" into the project. Perhaps you want to extract and examine all the tasks for which one office has responsibility to determine if the reason behind that situation needs your attention.

Becoming an exemplar for managing multiple projects to your office heads and project managers is a huge dividend of conducting the IPRs using this technique. Every meeting is an opportunity to mentor your team on effective management of multiple, complex, and long-range projects.

## Creating Change

As senior leader in an organization (office, division, or corporation), you have the opportunity; hopefully the capability; and definitely the responsibility to identify the shortcomings your organization needs to address, or new directions it must pursue.

Projects and initiatives, especially those that require changes in values or behaviors, are not 'fire and forget' events. Like turning the first spade in the groundbreaking or cutting the ribbon on a new facility, announcing the change is just one indicator the work has begun.

How do you as a senior executive ensure actions are being taken throughout the organization to embrace the change?

There are several actions you can take to increase the probability of success. Appeal to the logical and emotional aspects of the initiative. Include metrics in the routine meetings with direct reports and in performance appraisals; and include information about the initiative in every meeting you convene with parts of the organization. (See the paper waste story in Chapter 7.)

One of the best ways for leaders to ensure everyone is thinking about the initiative is to ask about activities and progress at every meeting. General questions should be followed up with specific inquiry lines to ensure all levels of your team understand the change; they understand the reason driving the change; are keeping their subordinate levels informed; and are taking concrete actions to support the initiative.

Chapter 2 will expand your understanding of task analysis and provide additional insights into developing a plan. It will also introduce you to a method of increasing the knowledge, skills, and abilities (KSA) of your teams in analyzing tasks and developing plans, while shortening the time required in developing robust plans of action.

## Learning from Executing

Too often, the issues that teams encounter, problems that are solved, and beneficial methods that emerge are lost to the team tasked with the next project. As the senior leader, you must plan for the capture of the good ideas thereby extending the memory of the project team. You must instill a consciousness for making observations, recording good practices, and making incremental improvements throughout the execution of a project.

You should begin each project by announcing your commitment to improving, avoiding the unsatisfactory practices, and capturing the good ideas. Robert L. Jackson began every project with this challenge, **"The After-Action Report starts now!"**

# Chapter 2

# Task Analysis and Planning

*Prescription without diagnosis is malpractice.*

Mature organizations adopt processes to ensure planning teams evaluate activities and events from multiple perspectives. Each of these viewpoints provides insight to help shape the plan. A shortcoming or misstep in a previous effort may have prompted the project manager to search for ways to ensure a more robust, informed analysis in the future.

Three techniques for task analysis are included here. If your office uses a different technique, one that works in your industry, there will be no attempt to dissuade you from using it. On the contrary, the goal in this chapter is to encourage you to adopt the rigor of a structured process, while discouraging you from what one colleague called stream-of-consciousness planning.

## Display Methods for Management and Progress

In understanding the analysis tool, you should differentiate the process of analysis and planning (which helps you uncover and organize the tasks) from the management tool used to display those activities and relationships that track progress towards project completion.

Several tools are available to display progress and can be selected depending on the nature of the project: Program Evaluation and Review (PERT); Critical Path Method (CPM); and Gantt (named for Henry Gantt). Peter Drucker offers a short introduction to each of these tools in *Management*.

This chapter is not about exhibiting the information. The object for you here is to first engage the team in uncovering all the activities necessary for the project to succeed.

In the next chapter, however, you will be introduced to a display tool that can be used for executive-level managers. The tool eliminates the clutter inherent in a complex project and allows a project owner to significantly increase her performance in one of the four functions of management—control. This powerful, yet easy-to-learn and easy-to-use, tool allows the senior executive to effectively manage several projects simultaneously. Its simplicity allows it to be used for every small or large project.

## Analysis Tools

Kenichi Ohmae: "**Analysis is the critical starting point of strategic thinking.**"

Voltaire: **No problem can withstand the assault of sustained thinking.**

## SWOT

Some industries prefer SWOT analysis to weigh the company's strengths and weaknesses against potential opportunities and threats. It's a straightforward system used to take a strategic-level look at an initiative such as rolling out a new product or entering a new market. The team takes a realistic appraisal of the company's strengths and weaknesses, along with those of the competition, and then applies that information to the expected opportunities in and threats against the initiative.

## DOTMLPF - P

When the Department of Defense (DoD) introduces a program or fields a new weapons system, one method of evaluating the necessary changes that must occur within the organization is the DOTMLPF-P (pronounced Dot-Mill-P-F-P) assessment.

NOTE: Acronyms, abbreviations, and initialisms will be explained when introduced. I was once cautioned, ***never use inside jargon on outside audiences*** (without an explanation). There is a glossary that contains definitions if you need a quick reminder.

When a major change is planned in DoD, the DOTMLPF-P assessment has proven to be an effective tool for understanding the interrelated systems that must be considered, as well as ensuring that all internal offices with subject matter expertise (SME) are consulted.

This appraisal requires the team to identify the changes that must be made in:

- *Doctrine* (principles that guide how the organization operates and fights);
- *Organization* (the structural changes required to accommodate the product or initiative);

- *Training* (the additional training efforts that must be undertaken, to include how often—the periodicity—the training must be conducted to hold the requisite skills above an established threshold of proficiency);

- *Maintenance* (the requirements for changing or publishing a technical manual, and the description of the maintenance, troubleshooting, and inspection of the item);

- *Leadership and Education* (the additional information or skills leaders need to acquire, and how this will occur—self-study; formal schooling; or delivered by traveling trainers known as the new equipment training (NET) team;

- *Personnel* (the changes required in human resource publications, education thresholds, and job descriptions to support the initiative);

- *Facilities* (the requirements for constructing unique maintenance facilities to support a product such as a vehicle that withstands blasts from roadside bombs, or a laboratory for modeling and simulation); and

- *Policy* (possible requirements to approach Congress for a change in the law that provides authorities for expending funds, or for a change to DoD policy to accommodate a particular program.)

This assessment provides an inward look, primarily, revealing insights into changes that must be made within the organization. Of course, most planning requires a look at the situation through several different lenses. This is especially true of planning that involves competition—or combat.

## <u>METT - TC</u>

The U.S. Army incorporates several mnemonic devices to assist in conducting mission analysis and developing plans. Using them does not guarantee a good plan, but not using them will almost certainly guarantee omissions in your analysis. Using these memory aids ensures key factors are considered.

The most common process employed by the Army is summarized in the mnemonic, METT-TC. It can be used at all levels and informs an activity labeled the military decision-making process (MDMP). It guides the team through an evaluation of: Mission, Enemy, Terrain, Troops, Time, and Civil Considerations. In the hands (heads) of even a rookie team, employing this structure can quickly increase performance level, and the knowledge, skills, and abilities (KSA) of the team members. There are few analysis tools that can outperform it. Using this process reveals information in a much more systematic and robust way than the instinctive "gut" insight that replaces more formal, logical analysis in some organizations.

METT-TC has its roots in combat planning, but with just a few mental adjustments can readily serve any project team. This mechanism evaluates the requirements, threats, locations, people, time elements, and communities in which the project will be conducted. It can be used in military, academic, and civic organization settings. It is effective for anyone developing plans, from the most senior executive to the frontline supervisor levels.

The analysis, the discovery process, should be your primary step in investigating the issue at hand—the problem, the opportunity, or the initiative. The issue is approached in a holistic manner, structured to aggregate the task list that will be uploaded into the software tool for eventual display and management.

## Mission

METT-TC analysis begins with a careful study of the *Mission*, or task, or whatever name you apply to the object of the team's study. As you focus on this aspect, consider all the statutory requirements. What does the law require or prevent with regards to this project? If you have been directed to develop the plan by corporate headquarters, what corporate regulations apply? Are there specific requirements levied by headquarters? Statutory or **specified** requirements are those legal obligations, and corporate policies and directives, around which you must organize your thoughts to be in compliance and succeed in the project.

For example: If you wanted to start your own television station, your team must identify all the federal laws that govern broadcast transmissions, plus local laws for starting a business in the town in which you are going to operate.

### Why is it important to begin your evaluation from this point?

Identifying all the requirements demands rigor in the research by all members of the team. You would not want your team to discover a piece of information, six months into a plan, which disrupts the execution and should have been uncovered in the original task analysis.

After you have recorded all the written requirements, it's time to prospect for the knowledge and experience of the planning team to grow your task list with **implied** actions. There could be 5 to 10, and even more, implied tasks for every specified task. Every member of the team should evaluate each mandated task and ponder what additional activities the specified task creates for his, or her, section or office. The study will help each office determine its supporting plan for this initiative. (There will be more about this in the chapter on delegation.)

Directives provided orally from the senior leadership team should be considered as specified tasks, even if they aren't provided in writing.

Identifying the specified (statutory, written, or vocalized requirements), and the implied (derived from the specified by your team based on their knowledge, experience, and thoughtful analysis) tasks are critical steps. This process is crucial in creating shared understanding of all the tasks that must be included in the project plan. If pressed for time or you just want to highlight the most important tasks, you can take the evaluation further, identifying the critical or mission essential tasks from the list of specified and implied. The other tasks might increase the project's value or make a transition less disruptive, but mission-essential tasks are pass-fail activities.

You may want to bin the tasks or place each task in a generalized line of effort. This can also help in identifying the responsible party.

In analyzing the assignment to close the Army base and move to another city in Germany, the specified and implied tasks were legion.

The list you develop when identifying the specified and implied tasks will populate most of your plan. These are the activities you must manage. Additional requirements will be revealed as you evaluate the other topics of METT - TC.

> Chief Warrant Officer Michael Dozier, a seasoned professional, added a key element to documenting the organization's analysis. He required members of the team to identify the source of each specified task they had identified. Afterwards, the planning staff listed the sources beside each specified task, and even tallied the number of requirements from each source. This process served in some ways as the "Federalist Papers" later, when asked, "Who said the unit had to do that? How did the organization develop this course of action?" We could quickly refer to our records.

**Like high school math, it helps to show your work.**

## Enemy

After sufficiently exploring all facets of the required activities and assembling a comprehensive list of specified and implied tasks, begin evaluating the "E" in METT-TC—the *Enemy*. You might be surprised to see this as a topic in a project management book, but in this work *Enemy* has a different context. You will need to open the aperture a bit on the use of this term.

Of course, *Enemy* can literally mean an opposing military force, but in a larger sense, from the MDMP perspective, it can refer to a set of conditions over which you have little or no control. In strictly military terms, this will include the Weather, Enemy, and Terrain (WET). If you are interested in further explanation of the DoD evaluation of WET, an online search will provide you with in-depth discussions of each of these factors.

In a corporate setting, this might be where you look at the strengths and weaknesses of your competition and their historical responses to initiatives by competitors. Are they nimble, or do their bureaucracies and decision cycles render them vulnerable? (Can you envision how METT-TC would nest with your SWOT analysis?)

In developing an emergency response plan for a natural disaster—hurricane, tornado, flood, or fire—it should be easy to draw the parallels as you plan for your hometown.

## Terrain

The next topic is actually embedded in the WET mnemonic—*Terrain*.

Several U.S. Army facilities were being vacated by units returning to the United States. Each was assessed for the base closure project. Each base was evaluated on several factors in addition to the most obvious of 'Can the facilities adequately house the headquarters, company offices, and soldiers?'

The primary tenant of the base being closed, one of three tenant organizations, was looking for a U.S. facility close to an airport suitable for rapid deployment, and to support their unique training needs. One method of infiltration used by the organization was parachute insertion. The training requirements for this unit from a terrain / location perspective demanded nearby drop zones (large, relatively flat fields devoid of obstacles). This, in turn, would necessitate future expansion of training infrastructure through contracting with private landowners for authorization to use their land for parachute operations. Were there adequate open spaces available near the base, unencumbered by commercial flight paths? Were there airports nearby?

The unit required large bodies of water to support the teams that approached their targets underwater or by surface craft. Also investigated were established ranges for rifle, mortar, and demolition training, and their relation to each base under consideration. Satisfactory ground transportation routes to facilitate easy travel to the major training areas located in Germany was also a factor. These and many more aspects were evaluated for each base offered.

If you were moving a corporate plant, or constructing a factory from scratch, you would also evaluate the transportation network—ground, air, and maritime—that would support the new facility. How close are you to airports, container seaports, highways, and rail lines?

Another area that can be evaluated as you analyze 'enemy' are the national and local laws, and other internal restrictions that tend to make coordination and execution more difficult. This may take the form of a protocol for meeting with government officials when you plan to expand operations in a foreign country. Arranging such meetings may take significantly longer than expected. Furthermore, it is highly unlikely you will walk away from the first meeting with a signed agreement, so you must plan for multiple meetings with various layers of officials.

Perhaps the bureaucracy of both parties, yours and the country in which you are moving, is your enemy—things not under your control. Maybe the permit to build must be approved by the mayor's committee, which only meets once a month. Part of evaluating the enemy would include identifying the meeting dates and protocols for becoming part of the agenda.

### Troops…your people, partners, and customers

The next subject in METT-TC reminds us to think about the *Troops*—the employees, your partners, and your customers; those who will be doing the heavy lifting or supporting your project. How will the project affect them and what actions will they need to take to support the plan? What actions will you need to take to ensure your troops are kept informed and their concerns considered in the planning and execution? You'll want to include the personnel who don't work for you but will provide support to your project. These could include people internal to your organization or, as in the case of the move in Germany, the local government leaders on both ends of the move. If you are engaged in a move, you should also cultivate a good relationship with the moving companies.

The move to other cities in Germany, spurred by the base closure, exceeded the capacity of all local moving companies. Moving companies were—to borrow an idea from Eliyahu Goldratt from his work on the theory of constraints—our weakest link, and it was something out of the unit's control (i.e., the enemy). The bottleneck was the limited pool of moving vans and labor for packing out the families and delivering their furniture to housing near the new base.

There was no room in the schedule for slowing down the move to accommodate a less aggressive movement plan. The base commander was turning over the keys to the front gate, the headquarters buildings, barracks, and the schools to the German government. Afterwards, there would no longer be American schools for children to attend. By the way, the plan included moving the schoolteachers who taught in the DoD school system. The movement planners and the movers had to work hand-in-glove. It was an example of tight coupling with very little slack.

Consider this situation: You've been holding on to personnel for the past year who should have already returned to the States because their three-year assignments in Europe were completed. But, because of a potential for war in the desert, the rotations back to the States had been frozen, while movements of personnel who were in the overseas assignment's pipeline to combat units had remained apace.

In normal times, rotations and assignments within the military are staged to flow at a consistent rate. This allows the families to plan for the next assignment and to mentally prepare for the upheaval that comes with every move. This natural flow allows for a certain percentage of houses at a base to be available for incoming families. But, suddenly, the military freezes departures from combat units but continues to send replacements forward from schools and staff assignments to combat units. A situation develops very quickly in which you have many more families than available housing.

Fast forward into the summer after the war had ended, and you are confronted with another tough situation. All the moves returning families to the States, previously postponed, now begin to happen – immediately. The families in the middle of their assignments must pack and move to the new base. All the replacements who had arrived during the past year and found no available military housing are living off-post in German rental properties at the original base. They are now uprooted a second time to resettle at the new base.

As you evaluate the moving companies, you discover only a small portion is skilled, equipped, and licensed to provide overseas shipping support. These are involved in packing families returning to the U.S. Another set of moving companies can only move furniture from one town to another in Germany.

Moreover, the U.S. military base and buildings the planning team ultimately selected, and expected to be empty by spring were still occupied by the unit scheduled to return to the States. That organization had also deployed in support of DESERT STORM and was now returning from the war in Iraq and undergoing similar turmoil.

The original plan allowed for each Green Beret Operational A-Team to continue training at the original base until a scheduled date at which time the team would cease training. The families of that team would be packed and moved to the destination base the following week. The schedule allowed one week for families to settle into housing; and then the team would resume training.

Unfortunately, the war disrupted the start dates of the team relocations, along with the departure of the unit vacating the buildings at the receiving base. Fortunately, the families were able to respond to an updated schedule quickly after the unit returned from the war, in June. Military families are known for their resilience.

The organization, the individual members, and their families had learned to be flexible in light of rapid changes taking place due to the Gulf War, and the end of the Cold War.

## Civil Considerations

The 'C' reminds planners to include *Civil* considerations. Your project may occur in your hometown, in a different country, or even on a different continent. Regardless, in developing a comprehensive plan, you'll probably want some level of analysis of the civil interests and involvement. The infrastructure, culture, population, available housing, etc. may all be parts of this analysis.

For many projects, after you have completed the evaluation of these essential areas of concern, the identification of tasks, for all practical purposes, will be done. The burden will now shift to scheduling the activities you've identified.

## Time

The final 'T' refers to the *Time* element—scheduling the activities. Are there hard and fast completion dates for some activities you identified? The base commander had a confirmed date of July 15 for the closing ceremony. The unit began returning to Germany during the first week of June. That left the soldiers and families about six weeks to empty the offices and base housing (apartments) of U.S. and personal property.

## Developing the Schedule

During this part of the analysis, you begin to develop a timeline. In earlier studies of the task, you should have posted dates as they were established or revealed, such as the schedule for the mayor's committee meetings. Now it is time to give serious consideration to all dates identified on your timeline. You'll review the final completion date in the light of all supporting activities, meetings, site surveys, etc., and ensure sequential activities are grouped, discussed, ordered, and plotted.

Ultimately, every task your team has identified must be assigned a completion date.

Have you looked at the ultimate completion date of your project and worked in reverse to schedule all the activities your analysis has identified? This technique is known as the reverse-planning process. It is the key to the Gantt chart planning—begin with the end product and date of delivery. It is used extensively in planning airborne operations. You begin with the date and time of the parachute assault and seizure of a key objective. From there work in reverse order, identifying each required task all the way back to the point of receiving the mission.

When using the tool that will be introduced in Chapter 3, your team will identify the task and responsible office, or person, and assign a no-later-than (NLT) completion date. This arrangement makes it easy for you, the executive, to manage the execution of the project.

Activities you didn't identify in the initial analysis will most certainly surface during execution and will require scheduling. You will want (need) to capture these tasks on your master plan. Don't ignore them just because they have already been completed. Listing them will serve you in developing your D-day plan for the next project.

The internal order of some of your sequential steps may be reordered later in the project life cycle. A helpful step when developing the plan is to identify the time requirement for key tasks and annotate other activities that must happen before that particular activity can be commenced. Evaluate what other events will be relying on the completion of this task before that next task can be started, or completed. As the project owner, or manager, you'll want to squeeze as much of the buffer out of the plan, which team members are sure to have padded into their requirements. (Padding time into the plan doesn't mean your team members are evil; it's just human nature.) This is an insight Goldratt discusses in his book *Critical Chain*.

As suggested earlier, for some projects the planning phase is almost complete after identifying and scheduling all the tasks. But for most projects, there are decisions to be made; plans to be developed. In these situations, the planning team must consider all the information and prepare several courses of action to present to the decision maker, who may not have been involved when the alternatives were developed.

## Process

In a course produced by the Learning Company, Professor Michael Roberto, of Bryant University, discusses the decision-making process used by John F. Kennedy's administration when confronted with the Cuban Missile Crisis. The world was on the brink of war. His advisors—White House staff, DoD, Intelligence Community, and Department of State (DOS)—developed a plan that met U.S. goals and moved both sides, the U.S. and USSR, away from war.

One reason this event serves as a great study is that it occurred only 18 months after a disastrous decision by the administration to attempt to overturn Cuba's Castro regime in an incident known as The Bay of Pigs invasion.

What had changed in the administration's decision making? Professor Roberto explains after the Bay of Pigs event, JFK invited former President Eisenhower to meet with him. Eisenhower, when serving in uniform, had been the architect of the D-day invasion of Normandy, France. One might suspect Ike would seize the opportunity to provide advice on estimating the size of landing force, location of assault beaches; calculating the requirements for fighter aircraft cover supporting the invasion; etc. Instead, Ike asked about the young president's decision process.

In the post-mortem of the Bay of Pigs decision, one of the issues identified concerned the planners who had overseen the training of the Cuban exiles. They were serving in advisor roles to the president. Those who had trained the exiles were in positions to counsel the president on the decision to launch the force, and inform him of the likelihood of success. Because of their attachment to the plan, they had strong personal interests in seeing the mission executed. This shortcoming was identified and eliminated in the newly adopted decision-making process.

Deming: **"We should work on our process, not the outcome of our processes."**

When the Cuban Missile Crisis occurred, the administration was ready to plan. The planning team moved from the White House to a site with less weight for the discussions. JFK removed himself from the day-to-day activities thereby reducing the inhibition in the team members in discussing facts, opinions, and alternatives.

Robert Kennedy, the president's brother, served as the devil's advocate and chief of staff to ensure the analysis and planning were thorough. Representatives from the different departments of government were assigned to teams, with each team tasked to develop a course of action. The course of action recommendations were exchanged so that the teams were evaluating plans they had not prepared - plans in which they had no personal stake.

Eventually, the teams working on the Cuban missile situation settled on a blockade as the solution, and it worked. If you are in the business of making tough decisions, invest time in listening to the series of lectures published by The Great Courses, entitled *The Art of Critical Decision Making*, by Professor Michael A. Roberto.

There are other steps within the military decision-making process. That's a topic you can research online. The goal in this chapter is to encourage you to adopt a structured analysis protocol to begin your planning, every time. You will be in the minority when you accept this challenge.

Here's an idea you may find worthwhile. Conduct the systematic analysis using the METT-TC process. Afterwards, use the DOTMLPF-P evaluation to understand what changes will be required internally to your organization.

## What if…?

During your project planning, consider how your organization will respond if the initiative is surprisingly successful, or your competition is uncharacteristically fast in launching a response. Look at the areas where potential issues may arise, and apply a few "What ifs?" Plan for the best case and the worst case; *Find out where 'Murphy' lives*. (From Murphy's Law - Whatever can go wrong, will go wrong, at the worst possible time.)

Here's a dilemma to consider. Even though DoD has an established procedure for task analysis, some organizations neglect to use it consistently. Employing the planning convention of METT-TC is not a discipline all have acquired. Much like performing daily maintenance and inspections on your fleet of corporate vehicles, or eating healthy and getting plenty of rest, METT-TC is **always endorsed, but rarely enforced.**

One seasoned officer would often ask young staff officers, "Do you use METT-TC to conduct analysis?" They invariably answered in one of two ways. The most common was, "Formal analysis (using the METT-TC process) takes too long". The other answer was, "We always use it".

But as Deming would say, **"If you don't not know how to ask the right question, you discover nothing."** This seasoned officer had learned years ago, while being on the receiving end of tough questions, not to be satisfied with the first answer.

## It Takes Too Long

His follow-up questions to the first response - "It takes too long" was "How long does it take?" Or, "Did you ever time yourselves to see how long it took?" and "How long is too long?" Without dragging you through the whole Socratic conversation, the young officer eventually admitted they didn't know how long it would take because they've never actually used it… "because it takes too long."

This response may remind you of the experiment in which hungry chimpanzees are placed in a cage with fresh bananas. As one hungry chimp, quite naturally, goes for the bananas, all the chimps are all hosed down with ice cold water. Another chimp tries to get a banana, with the same result. Eventually, they all learn, **"Don't eat the bananas."**

In continuing the experiment: One chimp after another is replaced. As each new and unsuspecting chimp (think new hire) goes for the bananas, it is beaten by its fellow chimps until it too learns not to eat the bananas. Finally, the replacement process is complete and none of the chimps left in the cage have been subjected to the water treatment. It is no longer necessary to use the water treatment because when a new hungry chimp is introduced to the group and goes for the bananas, the more experienced chimps in the cage administer the beating and the lesson. **"Don't eat the bananas."**

It may be in many organizations senior executives are confronted with the same mindset of those chimps. However, instead of avoiding the bananas, or having been punished with ice water, their staffs have heard repeatedly that detailed analysis "takes too long" so "Don't eat the bananas!"

## We Always Used It

The other common response to the seasoned officer's line of questioning was "We always use it". Again, he would fall into that annoying habit of asking follow-up questions. He had, undoubtedly, learned from senior leaders to use this technique to uncover the issues and discover the ground truth on initiatives.

He would continue his line of inquiry by asking the young officers to discuss *how* they used METT-TC. He would offer that he had seen analysis and planning in many organizations, and they all seem to have different techniques for employing METT-TC. "Talk me through your organization's process for conducting the METT-TC analysis." Very quickly, it would become apparent if the respondent was conversant in the analysis or had no insight into the process gained from actual experience.

Deming is quoted as saying, **"If you can't describe what you are doing as a process, you don't know what you're doing."**

After working with Bob Jackson, members of his staff had no trouble explaining the process, step by step.

Jackson's process with a few key additions was used in the Special Forces headquarters, Germany. Several significant adjustments to the process were introduced by the commander of the Green Beret unit, Colonel Stan Florer.

The thorough understanding one develops by using the same process for every project you confront - simple or complex - day in and day out, becomes part of your DNA. By establishing habits about the way you think, the pathways across the synapse become highways. The grooves become deeper.

## Develop the Staff and the Skills

Before leaving this Chapter, it's important to understand the process it took to metamorphose a staff that conducted 'adequate' study of an issue to one that engaged in comprehensive analysis. Their planning efforts moved up the scale from good to great.

In this chapter, you will be introduced to the process—a process you can employ—to educate and train your planning team in conducting comprehensive analysis.

You will ride along on a short trip to learn how a planning team progressed from requiring four hours to develop an adequate plan to acquiring the expertise necessary for conducting a no-notice, one-hour planning huddle that ended with a comprehensive plan for sending a Special Forces company into a remote region on the border of Turkey and Iraq, a mere four hours later. But this is stuff for later in the chapter.

## Inclusive brainstorming

As the organization approached closing a base in a town where there were established friendships and business linkages over 50 years, the senior executive—Colonel Darrell Katz— used a unique approach to inform the planning. It can be referred to as *inclusive brainstorming*.

The core planning staff had completed the structured analysis using METT-TC. Katz, the base commander, directed them to convene what would be called focus groups in a corporate setting. He wanted the spouses to have a voice in identifying tasks the staff would need to research and act upon. Katz also invited U.S. civilians (Army retirees still living in the area) to meetings designed to canvas them for their ideas and concerns. Many of these retired Green Beret veterans were filling positions necessary for operating the military base.

COL Katz included local German government and business leaders in the planning process. He engaged families with special needs children, the Post Exchange (military department store) and the commissary (military grocery store) personnel. He included people who ensured the security of the weapons, oversaw the maintenance of the vehicles, and several other interest groups and factions. Each of the groups identified tasks from their unique perspective the core planners would never have considered.

Although the focus groups provided the insights, the core staff (the project team) was tasked to ensure those concerns were included in the base closure plan, and all the activities were accomplished. Routinely, all the disparate groups were brought together to discuss the progress and learn of the answers that had been discovered. COL Katz conducted Town Hall meetings to keep the community at large informed of the progress of the move all along the way. Open communications, to all stakeholders, was essential in separating unfounded rumors from facts. Katz addressed and thereby eliminated the rumors. He was known for providing the unvarnished truth about the progress of the move.

Engaging with focus groups, seeking input outside the core planning cell, and showing interest in the concerns and suggestions undoubtedly removed the reluctance of the audience to introduce concerns and ideas to the project team.

One of the issues surfaced by a focus group member dealt with the massive safes and security containers in which classified documents are stored. The safes were extremely heavy. Not all were slated to occupy ground floors of buildings. As a result of this concern, civil engineers were brought in to evaluate the structure of the upper floors of the buildings at the destination.

Without tapping into the expertise of others not routinely included as core planners, this task in all likelihood would not have been identified until late in the execution phase. It could have resulted in a safety issue that stopped the move in its tracks. One mentor explained your team may have 99% of the information to run a successful project, but the 1% you don't uncover could be what derails it. Often someone in the organization knows the 1% but they aren't included in the planning because outside insights aren't actively sought or encouraged.

### Information Gaps

As planners investigate the objectives of a project, they will often discover gaps in the information and requirements that need to be addressed. This organization developed a simple method of processing the unknowns and the support requirements. They made several lists, posted them for all to see, and published the answers and decisions as they became available.

Requests for Information (RFIs) were used to fill knowledge gaps. Requests for support (RFS) encompassed a myriad of support activities. Request for funding (RF$) reflected the estimated costs for capital improvements to the buildings that would be occupied, and the costs of repairs to the buildings being returned to the German government. RF$ also included projected travel-related expenditures for surveying the destination base. RF$ identified the price tag for conducting the project, especially the amount that exceeded a normal operating budget.

In developing combat-focused plans and those plans to support the civilian community during natural disasters, planners routinely use a list identified as Requests for Forces (RFF). These reflect their understanding of the additional people (individuals or maneuver units) and capabilities (aircraft, tanks, etc.) that will be needed to succeed in a combat environment.

You've now reviewed the description of structured analysis as it is conducted. You may be thinking, "I agree with the young staff officers, this process looks too cumbersome to employ for real world projects and for it to be useful." Rest assured, it works in practice and your project team will produce a much better product, more quickly, by adopting the formal task analysis—SWOT, DOTMLPF-P, or METT-TC.

## How Do You Get Faster and Better?

How does that happen for an office? How do you get faster and better? How do you ensure everyone on the team understands the process?

Archilochus: **"We don't rise to the level of our expectations; we fall to the level of our training."**

The knowledge and skills needed to analyze a complex task thoroughly, and develop comprehensive, effective plans are acquired in the same way a musician learns to play an instrument, or athletic teams perfect their drills.

Imagine the young musician who, for the first time, picks up an instrument and tries to play a scale. Positioning of the fingers is uncomfortable; remembering where to place them is not automatic. It is a slow and onerous work. But with disciplined practice by the young musician under the tutelage of a seasoned music teacher, the student's fingers quickly learn their way around the instrument with a much higher degree of comfort. And with continued practice and coaching comes speed and improved quality. This illustration explains how analysis and planning can become quick and comprehensive.

Goethe: **Everything is hard, before it is easy**.

The staff inherited by Colonel Stan Florer, commander of the 1st Battalion 10th Special Forces Group, in Bad Tölz, Germany, could genuinely be called a team of rookies. Most members of his planning staff—the project management team for every project or mission the organization would undertake—had not previously worked in a staff position.

By institutional design, most personnel had spent the early years of their Special Forces careers carrying a rucksack and rifle, honing their skills for combat operations. Most Green Berets are loath to leave the operational A-team and become a member of the staff. These officers, warrant officers, and noncommissioned officers (NCOs) were seasoned professionals, but novices at working on a staff.

As part of their professional development and preparation for more complex combat planning, Florer scheduled an exhaustive talk through, walk through, and run through by the members of the staff. He used a straight-forward notional mission for the training exercise. The core planners identified to the assembled staff their requirements to support this operation.

Talking through the project from the perspectives of the different staff sections—human resource, intelligence, operations, readiness, training, logistical support, etc.—required several hours. One team member who had worked on more complex projects in past assignments was Chief Dozier, mentioned earlier. During the talk-through session, he provided insights from his experiences. Of course, Stan Florer also weighed in with his recommendations and requirements.

The staff officers and NCOs had learned about analysis using METT-TC in the Army's formal education program. That knowledge colored their discussions of activities, and their plans. Stan Florer added one element that increased the effectiveness of their analysis exponentially. He required the staff to systematically evaluate every topic represented by the letters in METT-TC, versus intuitively relying on the concept of METT-TC. This minor adjustment proved to be another number in the combination that unlocked the door to excellence in planning.

As a result of approaching METT-TC systematically, the staff's analysis now resulted in comprehensive, and not just robust, plans. Florer required his staff to use formal task analysis for every project undertaken. Obviously, the excuse 'it takes too long' fell on deaf ears with Stan Florer.

As his staff talked through each topic represented by METT-TC, the information was recorded by scribes—young officers and noncommissioned officers who weren't part of the core planning staff. This responsibility provided them insight into the comprehensive analysis used at the higher levels of the organization.

As the core planners talked through their thought processes and vocalized how each office would support the project, everyone on the team appreciated the impact and support that would be provided by the various offices. This had the bonus of preparing the next generation of staff officers. The assistants on the staff became intimately familiar with the thoughts of the primary staff members. This open discussion of implied tasks prepared the junior officers to step into the roles of primary staff when normal personnel rotations resumed. The scribes were more prepared to participate as a core planner as they progressed from Special Forces team members to staff officers. They also became better planners at the team level.

This method of talking through your thought process is used by hospitals in training medical staff. Young doctors and nurses gain insights by shadowing seasoned doctors on their rounds. During an examination, the doctor voices his or her thoughts generated by the patient's condition and response to treatment—thoughts informed by the doctor's experience.

### Returning to the planning exercise…

After investing the greater part of the day talking through the planning for a simple operation, the unit adjourned. Later, a smaller team of trainers convened to evaluate what was learned, and to schedule the next session.

A few days later, the staff and leaders from the subordinate offices, assembled again and applied the process to another, more complex, mission. The staff officers were a bit more polished in their roles, and much more fluent in the activities that must occur in their offices to support this, or any, project. Again, after developing a plan, the organizational staff adjourned, reviewed, and scheduled the next session.

Several days later, the team assembled and conducted analysis on an operation that was much more complex. Colonel Florer eliminated the luxury of unlimited time for analysis and planning. As an additional objective in the training, he established an artificial time requirement to present the plan to the boss in two hours.

The time constraint eliminated much of the philosophy discussions and war stories that can creep into any assembly of professionals. In addition, at this juncture, the attendees were much more familiar with the common requirements their offices, and the others, would necessarily act upon for almost any project. They were able to finger the scales more quickly and with greater accuracy and confidence. The team became laser-focused on the specifics this particular mission would require.

Florer was now satisfied with the quality of the analysis, and the ability of the team to produce comprehensive plans in a time-constrained environment. The next step in the development of the staff was to present a complex problem with a short deadline and no prior warning—a no-notice exercise to the planning staff.

After this final training event, Stan felt the staff was ready. All other projects this team tackled over the next year were actual issues facing the organization. Some were internal initiatives, while others were assigned missions. They used the process on a daily basis when deployed to support combat operations during OPERATION DESERT STORM.

The staff developed confidence in the skills required for this aspect of their work. It paid off months later in Turkey. Florer and senior members were called into a general's office and presented with a situation requiring his staff to plan the employment of a Special Forces company, supporting Kurdish refugees.

Florer, and his team, departed the general's office at 3:00 a.m. with a short-notice mission. The first plane carrying SF soldiers had been scheduled to lift off at 7:00 a.m. This mission allowed only four hours to analyze the task, and the METT-TC considerations; develop a plan; and ensure the teams were ready (with the knowledge and equipment) to board the planes. These planes would take them to an area where 100,000 Kurdish people had established a tent city, and were dying at the rate of more than 100 every day.

The other companies deployed to or established camps soon after the short-notice departure of the first company. The Green Berets would spend the next 2 months living among the Kurdish people, caring for them, and ultimately returning them to their villages in Iraq. The teams were credited with saving thousands of lives.

### <u>The keys to effective task analysis and planning:</u>

- Adopt a structured analysis tool.

- Use inclusive brainstorming.

- Talk through the steps in analyzing a project.

- Talk, crawl, walk, and run through a few planning sessions.

This process will prepare you for the sprint that might be required when your competitor launches a product you weren't expecting, or your company experiences an industrial accident with environmental impact.

Aristotle: **"For the things we have to learn before we can do them, we learn by doing them."**

There are several more activities you'll need to include in your project plan. They will be discussed in later chapters. One is the unique key to executing your plan well, and one you'll find most managers neglect to include in the plan.

Two final quotes to consider about planning:

Von Moltke: **"No plan of operations extends with any certainty beyond the first contact with the main hostile force." This quotation is often summarized as 'no plan survives first contact with the enemy'.**

In casual conversation, General Frederick Kroesen, challenged this famous quotation. **"If you are developing plans for combat and they don't include what to do when you are getting shot at, it's not much of a plan."**

Be careful about buying into conventional wisdom or clichés.

Consider General Kroesen's advice when developing your corporate plans. If you don't consider your competitor's response, it's not much of a plan.

# Chapter 3

# Managing the Execution

In Chapter 2, you were guided through the process of analyzing the requirements of a project and developing a comprehensive plan. You were exposed to 'inclusive brainstorming' as practiced by Darrell Katz and provided a glimpse into the structured analysis technique required by Stan Florer. You were introduced to a technique for increasing the skill level of your team to analyze tasks and develop plans. Both Katz and Florer were great practitioners of the art and science of good management.

In this chapter, you will return to the mind and behavior of Bob Jackson; and the way he prescribed information to be presented in order to apply his management expertise to an issue. You will observe how he ensured every project was executed in a superior fashion. A short review of Jackson's background and unique brand of leadership will help you appreciate his methods.

### Colonel Robert L. Jackson

Colonel Jackson had served four years in combat. He was a battle tested and experienced leader. He had been graduated from a prestigious university. He held an advanced degree in Organization Effectiveness (OE). Jackson encouraged his leadership team to use the offices of the Army's OE staff to conduct climate surveys of their units. He wanted them to understand where the employees (troops) felt there were unsatisfactory situations, along with the unit's strong suits. He encouraged openness about discovering where problems existed, versus ignoring or hiding problems.

Another of Jackson's mantras was: **Fix the problem, not the blame**.

### Very Few Meetings

His management style was demanding but extremely effective, more coach than cheerleader. Jackson's schedule of meetings was minimally invasive. The leadership team was required to attend only two one-hour meetings each week. The goals of these two meetings were to understand how the organization was performing and identify where there were improvement opportunities; one conducted on Monday, the other on Friday.

Jackson also convened a very limited number of single-focus meetings (always tightly run) throughout the month where he evaluated the status of personnel turnover, professional development, combat readiness, or special projects.

Each of these special purpose meetings was scheduled for a specific time on a set day of the month. For example, the meeting focused on professional development and retention of younger soldiers was always held at 3 p.m. on the third Wednesday of the month.

This consistency allowed his leaders to plan their activities around an orderly calendar. He fiercely defended the schedule from disruptions imposed by 'corporate' headquarters. When senior executives above him announced meetings that conflicted with his department's schedule, he was never timid in suggesting a different time. Jackson had **the back*ground* and the back*bone*** to point out the adverse impact of short-notice meetings on subordinates' plans and insist on deconfliction of schedules.

One of the keys he employed to manage the white space on his calendar (keeping his free time free) was personally identifying the processes that needed to be managed and allotting time on the calendar for each one. He recognized that **you either manage the calendar or it manages you**. Using this time to identify areas of excellence and shortcomings enabled Jackson to capitalize on successes, and ensured he was rarely surprised by disappointing performance in any system. His extensive academic and professional background equipped him to identify the key activities a large organization must execute well. He developed a rhythm in these efforts over time as he became sensitized to the frequency needed to optimize his time on each system.

## Spinning Plates

His management technique might be compared to the art of plate spinning, that classic stage act of keeping multiple plates spinning on tall, slender poles. The skill in the performance is to move from plate to plate, giving each the necessary attention to maintain the spinning motion that keeps it in balance.

The spinning plates of organizational systems are more complex. Because each plate has a distinct mass and spin factor, are not uniformly round, are perched on dissimilarly-sized poles, and have unique relative values to the organization each demands different levels of attention.

Jackson had honed his knowledge, skills, and ability (KSA) to the point he understood the frequency, amount and type of pressure to apply to each system (plate) to maintain its equilibrium. Some processes needed his attention daily, some only once a week and still others just once a month. He was also quick to make the necessary adjustments when changes occurred in the experience and skill level of primary system managers due to personnel turnover.

Deming suggests: **You manage the cause, not the effect**.

Jackson counseled his direct reports to identify the individual activities they needed to manage (to a novice manager they seemed endless); the information to extract for his use; and the way information should be displayed to be most effective for him and higher-level managers. He invested time, up front, in creating the management system and helping his direct reports understand the reason each piece of data was important, and why it should be reported in a particular format. As a result, when provided information, he was able to quickly view the key points and understand the condition within each system in the organization. He did this without having to search through each office's report for the nuggets of information critical to managing.

## Meeting Discipline

In meetings that lack discipline in reporting critical information in a succinct way, managers can find themselves listening to seemingly endless conversations about issues without uncovering any useful data.

Jackson required the data to be displayed and discussed at meetings. Instead of reviewing the data in the quiet of his office, he allowed his subordinates a peek inside the mind of an astute senior manager. In this way, he contributed to their professional development. Participating as observers gave them great insight into an executive's use of information to manage large, complex organizations.

The organization of his calendar, and personal discipline in managing his time (activities), allowed him to plan, organize, and control the activities of the organization with the minimum expenditure of time. All the while, he was maximizing his available time for visiting training, mentoring his direct reports, and imprinting his stamp of excellence on the unit (leading the organization).

This is how Jackson executed the four functions—plan, organize, lead, and control—of management. There will be additional discussion about a system approach in a later chapter, but for now the focus will be on investigating how Jackson managed special projects.

## A Manager's Responsibility

It might be helpful to remind yourself of the shared value of personal responsibility, which he embraced. The value, simply stated, is: As a manager, everything your organization does or fails to do is your responsibility. In that vein, he ran the organization as if it were a business and he were the owner, the sole proprietor. No task that members of the organization did—to include sliding under a vehicle to determine the source of an oil leak—was beneath him. This willingness to directly participate in even the dirtiest jobs in the organization was simply one way of assessing the organization, and should not be seen as an indicator of unwillingness to delegate. And Jackson was always looking for ways to build long-term value in the organization.

His brand of leadership would not be comfortable working with a leader who bragged that he had never visited the shop floor – the production facility; that he could manage the organization from reports and charts without interacting with the rank-and-file employees.

Jackson loved and respected soldiers and he loved soldiering. Like other leaders introduced in this book, his paramount motivation seemed to be service to the nation. For him, building long-term value in the organization was more than a local commitment. This value involved increasing the expertise in his leadership team for service to the nation for the next decade and beyond.

## Meetings and Execution

The meetings Jackson chaired were convened—as he was quick to say—"for *his* benefit". They were designed to provide information to him so he could manage the organization. These meetings weren't opportunities for extraneous conversation or visiting with a buddy who worked in another division of the business.

Conversation during the meetings was generally limited to reporting the status of activities for which you were responsible and responding to probing questions asked by Jackson. This is not to indicate communications in the organization were stifled, but jocular conversations were held before and after the meetings, or throughout the week, not when Jackson was gathering his data. He respected the time you were devoting to this meeting.

Although the formal meetings were highly structured to achieve clear objectives, outside of meetings he was always approachable and open for conversations and advice about any aspect of work. There were also allowances for a healthy amount of humor inside the conference room.

Bob Jackson, in managing projects, had no peer. As reported in the opening dialogue, Jackson would begin every project announcing, **"The After-Action Report starts now!"**

## After-Action Reports

A word about After-Action Reports: When conducted, an after-action review (the meeting(s) used to gather information for the after-action report) is usually the last action an organization would execute in a project, often an afterthought. Not so, with Jackson.

He would urge everyone to segment a portion of their notebooks for observations and lessons learned. He insisted it was important when confronted by a good idea, or a shortcoming, to write it down immediately. He often exclaimed, **"A short pencil is better than a long memory".** Or he might say it differently, **"a dull pencil is better than a sharp memory".** A Chinese proverb conveys a similar message suggesting the superiority of the "faintest ink" against "strongest memory".

## Management Activities Embedded in the Project Plan

After the planning team had identified and arranged all the tasks, Jackson would add another layer of activities to the plan. These were his management activities. He would schedule status reports—in-progress reviews (IPRs)—routinely through the project. If it were a long-range project, with a completion date one year or more in the future, he might convoke monthly reviews. As the project completion date grew closer, he would convene meetings every other week. When the completion date was only one week away, he required a daily update (stand-up meeting) to discuss all the tasks to complete as the project was finalized.

## A Golden Nugget Concerning Execution and Status Report Meetings:

Schedule the completion dates, the no-later-than (NLT) dates for an activity, on the day preceding the day of the week when you meet for in-progress reviews. If your meetings are on Fridays, schedule the NLT dates for close of business on Thursday.

He had discovered team members often fall into the trap of waiting to work on a task, scheduled for completion that week, until the day it is due. As is often the case, as one begins to work on it, the task turns out to take longer than suspected. At other times, team members get involved in urgent tasks that must be dealt with immediately, or the office with which coordination must be made is not available that day or week.

Eliyu Goldratt, in his management novel *Critical Chain* might have considered this falling prey to the term paper mentality, and buffer management.

Subsequently, the project team attends the meeting that afternoon and a member must report "the task isn't complete, yet", but offers, "It will be complete before we leave this evening." If the meeting date is scheduled on the NLT date, that seems to be a satisfactory answer.

But sometimes, in spite of good intentions, the task is not completed that afternoon. Nor is it completed the next day. In fact, it may be several days before the team members return to the task. In an even worse case, it may not be completed in time for the next meeting.

As the senior executive, an effective way to eliminate this excuse is to schedule your task completion dates at least one day before your meetings. When receiving the status report: accept only 'yes it's completed' or 'no, it's not' as answers. (In fact, 'no' is never a satisfactory answer when you are managing a project). As Jim Rohn suggests about answers to questions, and I'll paraphrase, **"The box is small. I can only fit a yes or a no. If it's a yes, no discussion is necessary and if it's a no, I understand the reason for that answer, too."**

Be very clear to your team members that you (the senior executive) are the project owner. Team members must notify you, along with the project manager, and your deputy, early in the week (or in the project life cycle) if the task is not going to be completed on time.

Team members must seek assistance early. If someone surprises the team with an announcement, they haven't completed their task, you might consider making it a teaching point: *Everyone is depending on all members to get their tasks completed on time.* In a project, no one is acting in isolation.

## No Excuse Management

What if you reported to your boss there wasn't enough time to complete one of the tasks that week, but her response began with a reminder to you the project is 6 months old? Instead of understanding the overwhelming events of this week, her reply was, "You've had 6 months to complete this task." It would be hard to argue with that kind of logic. Instead of looking at the task and the understandably limited time between in-progress reviews, the effective manager calculates available time from the start date of the project. You should adopt that mindset. Calculate the time required to complete a task from the start date.

The necessity for making corrections a second time would be rare for a no-nonsense manager like her. As the project owner, refuse to accept failure. Refuse to accept, "It will be done by the end of the day." The agreed upon date was yesterday! Remember, no one likes to be the center of attention for correction. View the plan and its timeline as a contract among the team members and ensure they do likewise.

If, on the other hand, this shortcoming becomes a routine for one of your direct reports, you'll have to spend some time coaching. You might have to spend time counseling. But, by and large, everyone wants to do a good job. No one wants to look bad in front of the boss, or their peers. Team members tend to respond well to good coaching, and quickly learn to manage their time and apply their focus better when high standards are upheld.

When substandard performance continues despite your corrective efforts, it might be a situation where you should meet with the offending party and discover how they are going about their work. Perhaps they need help but aren't comfortable asking for it. In the case of someone new to the job, it could mean he or she isn't ready for the additional responsibility. Don't rule out other causes as you investigate. Perhaps there is a personal situation impacting your subordinate's performance. Whatever the reason, you must identify and resolve it to ensure every team member is contributing effectively to the project.

## The Vehicle Fleet Maintenance Supervisor

One colleague tells the story of an exceptionally competent and effective maintenance supervisor. Asked how he kept the organization's diverse fleet of vehicles on the road with up-to-date services, even though many of his mechanics were new hires, he provided a number of enlightening observations.

The supervisor explained when a freshly-trained mechanic arrives, "he may understand how to check fluids and replace parts, but won't know how each vehicle fits into the action plan for the organization." That is management's job! Thus, the new mechanic won't know when the section must surge to ensure every vehicle is available, or when a particular vehicle can be taken out of service for major overhaul and maintenance.

But as the mechanics gain experience they will learn how to organize the work to best support the organization. Until then—and this was his secret—"**I put them on my schedule.**" He tells them which vehicle and why…why that vehicle, why today and why it goes to the front of the line for service.

As an experienced mechanic, the supervisor also had a fair sense of how long each action should take for a novice, and how quickly an experienced mechanic should complete the same work. He knew how closely he should watch a procedure, and which processes he could inspect after they were complete.

As mechanics became more experienced and showed a sufficient level of competence and commitment, the supervisor would allow them more leeway in making the decisions about what tasks they would perform that day, and in what order.

We return to managing the project…

## The Display and Progress Management Tool

You'll find the tool introduced here is deceivingly simple. It's easy to learn. It's easy to populate with every task. And most importantly, as the project owner and senior executive, it's easy to read and see the critical information immediately. And if all project leads use this format, you can merge the management of all your projects into combined IPR meetings with those project leads.

Consider the tool you are using to display the information and track progress. Is there a training course specifically designed to develop competence or expertise in the tool? Is everyone on the team - from novice to master - trained to use the tool? Or, on the other hand, are only one or two members of your team skilled in the use of this tool? Why not everyone? Is it too costly to send everyone to attend the course?

With the tool recommended here, you won't have to send someone to an expensive course to learn how to employ it or manipulate the data in it. Everyone can learn how to use it in only a few minutes.

Unfortunately, there can be a reluctance to use it. People often fall into the trap of using a complex software tool that does a great job for many aspects of project management but isn't user- or executive management-friendly.

This tool, known by various names - Milestone Chart, Master Sequence of Events List (MSEL...pronounced mee - zel) or Plan of Action, and Milestones (POA&M) - is organized to provide the project owner the following information:

Due Date
Project name
Task
Responsible person or office
Notes

| NLT | Project | Task | Responsible | Notes |
|-----|---------|------|-------------|-------|
|     |         |      |             |       |
|     |         |      |             |       |

Table 1

The matrix is usually prepared using a 'landscape' layout. Each column is discussed below.

If all projects for which you are responsible are organized in this format, they can be blended and sorted as needed for you to monitor the on-time completion of all tasks. You can also ensure your team is looking ahead at the tasks on the horizon.

## Plan of Action and Milestones

The No-Later-Than (NLT) time indicates when the task must be completed, without fail, by the end of that workday. If the responsible party (column 4) sees an issue that can't be resolved and the task will not be completed, it's incumbent to notify the project owner, deputy, and project manager before the status meeting and not just a few minutes before the meeting. Senior personnel need to have adequate time to break through the logjam that is preventing completion.

There is a technique to vouchsafe success in an endeavor. It involves finding out early when someone who is doing their best is not going to achieve what is expected. Wouldn't it be helpful if the management team arranged support, providing help whenever some part of the organization is faltering, instead of discovering at the end of the quarter someone didn't make their production quota? The underpinning Jackson implemented had its roots in the same outfit made famous in the book and movie; *We Were Soldiers Once, and Young.* See Chapter 12 - Shortstop the Shortfalls, Managing for Success.

Column 2 identifies the various projects for which you are responsible. With the project title identified here, you know who is responsible for task completion of all activities in that project and to whom you would provide guidance on that project for the upcoming weeks.

The project leads can use this format by substituting the name of their phases or lines of effort within a project in the "Project" block under column 2.

Column 3 is fairly straightforward. Every task the planning team identifies during the task analysis is listed in this column, along with the management meetings (IPRs). All tasks due for completion before this meeting are displayed and discussed at the IPR. At the more senior executive levels, you will want the project leads to identify the key activities only, or summarize the tasks, versus identifying every action the team is working on or has completed.

## Who is responsible?

The responsible party is not Joe who works in marketing. Savvy managers only list their direct reports in the responsible party column. You, personally, should not care if the head of marketing assigns the task to Joe. As the senior leader and project owner, your major concern is the task is completed on time. If it is not completed, you must hold the marketing manager responsible, totally responsible, for everything the marketing division does or does not do.

If you hear, "I gave that task to Jane and she hasn't finished," understand the problem is not with Jane. The problem is with supervision of the task by the marketing manager. Your marketing manager may need help to strengthen his or her delegation skills to include the persistent follow up required when tasks are delegated; more on this in Chapter 8 - Delegation. All your direct reports need to understand from the start why only their names will appear in Column 4.

In the 'notes' column, you might consider identifying the connectivity of this task with others. You may include some insights to historical stumbling blocks. The time estimated for completing the task could be listed here. Perhaps the start time is recorded.

As you can see, this tool is very simple. The problem in displaying information for the manager often lies in the desire by well-meaning project managers to show the boss more information than needed or even to show all the information they have. You may have seen spread sheets with more than 20 columns, with 10 lines of text in some of the rows; each task and its rather lengthy explanation squeezed into a single spread sheet cell. The font in such documents is almost microscopic.

Tremendously complex spreadsheets increase the difficulty in managing the activity. Requiring the tasks within the POA&M to be succinct enough that it can be displayed on one screen forces the project manager and project leads to limit the words reflecting the task, and those responsible for the action. This is similar to the A3 requirement in lean processes.

## Brevity

A word about brevity: In the old days, Green Berets would send messages by radio and Morse code. Whoever wrote the message was obliged to crank the portable generator that powered the system. It was very easy to turn the handles until the communications sergeant began tapping out the message on the Morse Code key. When sending the message, the machine demanded a great deal of sustained muscle power to turn the crank. The writer quickly learned to be succinct in subsequent messages.

Too often, a novice senior executive will allow the subordinates to craft the tool or decide upon the information to be displayed. That is a rather large mistake because it results in the senior leader spending valuable time learning where to look for key information.

Subordinates often provide information important to their own offices, but they do not provide the executive with the key and essential information needed to manage the activities of the organization at large.

Additionally, if training is needed to view and decipher the information and tie the disparate pieces together to manage all the systems, it might be time to consider changing the management system.

There is a story about the first year Tom Watson, Jr. took the helm at IBM. It was a banner year with great sales. Unfortunately, he had to report 'no profit' at the annual stockholders' meeting. IBM had not managed expenses.

There might be new data and metrics a senior executive has not had to worry about in previous roles. But he or she would do well to give some thought to identifying the right information and the most effective way of delivery to them. As a senior executive, you want the information displayed for your benefit, not the benefit of the project manager. If you desire more understanding, arrange a deep dive where all the information is provided and discussed. Deep dives are particularly appropriate in situations when the project, the project manager, or the senior executive is new. Be ready to dissect and digest the information.

When artfully employed, you can manage multiple projects blended into one milestone chart using this tool. By extracting the tasks from each project and shuffling them in with the others according to date, the senior executive can manage multiple projects at one meeting. The more projects you can handle effectively, the greater your value to and potential in the corporation. Or as one friend advised a colleague who was lamenting the multiple projects in which he was engaged, **"No one pays to watch a clown juggle just one ball."**

One of the most endearing qualities of the tool is, like METT-TC, it can be used on the smallest project, like the company picnic, or the most complex. This is the tool the organization used to support the Kurdish refugees and this was the tool used to close the base and move to another city and state, in a foreign country.

## Lessons LEARNED - Tips, Observations, Insights, and Lessons Learned (TOILL)

Another set of entries Jackson would introduce on the milestones list were the lessons learned meetings. Routinely, throughout an extended project, or immediately following a short duration project, Jackson would devote one of his project status meetings to gathering observations and lessons learned.

After the POA&M was populated with the tasks identified during the METT-TC analysis, plus the management activities tracking those tasks, Jackson would add these tasks: after-action review; publishing the after-action report; changing the organization policy, if necessary; announcing the change to the policy; etc. He made learning and improving a part of every project. (There will be more about the Lessons Learned program later.)

## The In-Progress Review (IPR)…the essence of managing the project

The meeting would start exactly on time, every time. Jackson considered it rude to those who showed up on time to delay a meeting. Jackson's meetings ended on time, as well. The staff felt rushed to get through the information and gather his insights. As a result, no one ever felt the meetings were a waste of time.

The POA&M would be displayed. There would be a checkmark to indicate the task had been completed, or on rare occasions, some indicator the task was incomplete. Jackson would dig into the situation to determine why it wasn't complete and what resources needed to be marshaled to assist. If the tasks were all 'green' he might select a task, or two, to discuss and evaluate. He wanted to ensure tasks were completed but he also encouraged an exchange of ideas on how tasks had been approached or issues resolved.

Jackson would often jump ahead a few weeks or months in the schedule to discuss one of the future tasks about which he had concerns. He may have felt not enough time was being devoted to it now, early in the project, to ensure it would be completed by the due date. He invested in careful study of the project between meetings to identify key tasks to highlight and discuss.

When time permitted, Jackson would ask someone to share with the team some observations (lessons) they had recorded so far. The first time one hears that line of inquiry, rest assured your direct reports will spend part of each week searching for ways to improve the organizational processes. When called on by Bob Jackson, you didn't want to respond with a blank stare, as you stumble for words that suggested your inattention to his first entreaty, "The After-Action Report starts now!"

## Management by Walking Around

At one time, there was a technique in vogue called *management by walking around*. Managing a project isn't limited to attending progress report meetings. Managers need to be out and about checking to ensure the work is being done. Jackson and other leaders you'll meet in this book were committed to being out and about, among the soldiers. General Thomas H. Tackaberry, was famous for saying, **"If a leader spends more than two hours a day behind his desk, he's just plain lazy."**

Gerstner said, **"I have always believed you cannot run a successful enterprise from behind a desk."**

## How Management by Walking around Looked in Jackson's Unit

When you were on a rifle range with your company, you might get a call informing you Jackson was in the motor pool (vehicle parking lot and maintenance station) going over the maintenance records and activities.

When you were working with your mechanics, he might show up in the arms room (the room where all the weapons were stored).

When you were leading your soldiers on a 25-mile hike Jackson might arrive with his rucksack and hike right along with you, talking to soldiers and your frontline supervisors (the sergeants).

His genuine interest in all aspects of the organization, and in the welfare of the soldiers, had the effect of greatly increasing productivity.

For an interesting study on the impact of showing interest in your team members' jobs, check out the experiment that resulted in identifying the phenomenon known as the Hawthorne Effect. Understanding this effect on employees might have contributed to the motivation behind leaders in this book spending very little time in their offices dealing with their in-boxes. But the primary reason shown in multiple ways was their obvious enjoyment of associating with soldiers.

When Jackson visited, his conversation might be about one of the special projects, especially if the activities were being executed by members of the rank and file, the troops. This is one way he kept informed of the ground truth about the project status and knew questions to ask during the formal meetings.

He also enjoyed asking questions about the details of one's job, regardless of the person's rank or position. Sometimes he knew the answers and wanted to ensure you were hitting the books hard enough. His questions often drew out information you knew, but he would help you understand how it was connected to the larger effort. The conversation would influence you in applying that information to other aspects of your job, or other parts of the organization.

At other times, he asked questions because he truly didn't know the answer and wanted to increase his professional knowledge about technical issues; he was collecting data. He was always willing to listen and learn because it furthered his professional development as a leader.

In meetings, his questions might be intended to highlight your procedures because he wanted the others to learn and employ the same techniques. At other times, it was to help you understand you weren't managing the task with sufficient focus. You were letting things happen versus ensuring good things were happening.

## Senior Executive Norms

In the 82nd Airborne Division, junior officers, and junior noncommissioned officers (sergeants) and enlisted organization members are introduced to a behavior model of general officers—the senior executives—influencing expectations for senior managers thereafter.

## Management by Jumping In and Walking Around

During a training mission in the early 1970s, an airborne infantry company had conducted a night parachute assault to seize an airfield as part of a larger operation conducted by the battalion. (A company is roughly 150 soldiers; a battalion approximately 600.) The companies began moving toward outlying objectives with the intent of attacking *some disputed barricade.* (From Alan Seeger's poem) They had dropped in shortly after midnight and moved throughout the night to be in the assault position at first light.

At 3 a.m. (0300 hours), one young trooper observed a small team of soldiers moving about in the formation. The number of radio antennas suggested a senior officer was tagging along. The soldier asked his squad leader who they were.

It was his introduction to the commander of the 82nd Airborne Division, General Frederick Kroesen, a World War II, Korean War, and Viet Nam War veteran. As the trooper would find out, it was Kroesen's practice to participate in the parachute assault with a unit and move with them to evaluate their tactical discipline and prowess. He also used the opportunity to develop a general appreciation of the quality of leadership within the organization. He would move with each company some portion of the night.

Shortly before daylight, the commanding general would disengage and return to division headquarters so he could participate in physical fitness activities with other battalions.

His successors, generals like Tackaberry, J.J. Lindsay, and Guy S. Meloy, exhibited the same leader traits, spending significant amounts of time out of their offices and immersing themselves in the activities of the soldiers. They would routinely show up in the line at the mess hall (now politely referred to as a dining facility), motor pools, company headquarters, or the rigger shed (where parachutes are repaired and packed). There is no doubt the leaders in the 82nd are still cut from the same cloth today.

## Attending every meeting

One of the most valuable lessons Jackson taught, by personal example, was to show up for every meeting. He rarely tasked his '2IC'—second in charge—to chair his meetings.

Because of his personal commitment to chair each meeting, and his mandate for all direct reports to do the same, the team's focus on execution remained laser-like. Enthusiasm and zeal for the project remained constant because he made it clear beyond a shadow of a doubt, every project was important to him, and it should be to everyone else as well.

Conversely, you may have worked on projects that began with great fanfare and promise. But after a few weeks, the senior executive who launched the program would allow himself to become distracted and quit attending the meetings. He would begin to disengage by sending his second in charge. This apparent time-saving measure sends a loud and clear signal to everyone, and the results are always entirely predictable.

Soon, the direct reports quit attending and begin sending their deputies to 'take notes and keep me informed'. The routine meetings often are canceled at the last minute, resulting in a uniform loss of productive work by subordinates as they had kept that time blocked on their schedules. The energy loss becomes palpable; zeal for the project completely sapped; commitment levels lowered across the board.

Often the project is canceled or meets a slow death from lack of care and feeding. Occasionally, when failure is imminent or disinterest becomes so apparent even the disengaged manager is awakened to the situation, there might be a grand resurgence of activity and interest for a short time. But just as often, the plug is pulled on the initiative. Sadly, the manager doesn't understand why his team was ineffective.

Perhaps some managers believe projects can be launched like guided missiles, with a fire-and-forget mentality. All they need to do as the senior executive is identify the task, give an impressive speech, pull the trigger, and success is guaranteed. Unfortunately, that's not how projects or organizations succeed.

It's said if money were no object, resources unlimited, and no time constraint or competition, we wouldn't need management. But those conditions never exist. And, as the tree farmer suggests, **even a hole has to be managed.**

Jackson, by his personal commitment to lead, and unwavering devotion to disciplined management, made each project a lesson in organizational effectiveness and excellence.

You can too, by following his lead.

If you ensure all the activities are identified and listed in the correct sequence; you manage the list requiring the tasks to be completed by their no-later-than date, without fail; and your team completes all the individual tasks, to standard, within budget, how can you not achieve overwhelming success in every project you manage?

At this point in the discussion, you've seen how a few very talented senior executives analyzed a project, developed a plan, and managed the execution. The next chapter will help you understand with greater appreciation how a few high reliability organizations execute with excellence.

Words of encouragement as you go forward:

You may think the environment in which you work is so vastly different from those described here the lessons don't apply. I suggest the same principles are involved.

As the project owner, or senior executive you should:

- Ensure the project is thoroughly analyzed and organized with the tasks sequenced.

- Assign each task to someone who works directly for you.

- Ensure your direct reports understand you hold them responsible for completing the task on time.

- Encourage your team to look for ways to make improvements, even if only incremental.

- Get out of the office to check progress where the employees are doing the work. Don't rely solely on the meetings to determine how the project is progressing.

- Show interest in your employees' activities whether in a motor pool, where the code writers sit, on the loading docks, or on the shop floor.

- Stay engaged, attend the meetings, be prepared to ask questions.

- Execute with excellence.

- Reflect and learn from every project or experience.

This process works for those in uniforms or in a business suit. Walk the Gemba.

Colonel Arthur Stang of the 3rd Brigade of the 82nd Airborne Division, another genuinely gifted leader, kept a 3X5 card reminding him to stay in touch with the troops and get out of the office.

- **Have you talked to the troops today?**

- **Don't forget the wrench turners, and spoons. (*mechanics and cooks*)**

- **Remember, the only thing you lead from behind this desk is a pencil.**

A note to Project Owners: After the basic POA&M has been developed, task the members of your management team (your direct reports) to extract their tasks, evaluate each, and brief you at the next meeting on these kinds of issues:

- Which tasks will be the most difficult?

- Over which tasks do they not have 100% control?

- With whom will they need to coordinate and work?

Have them brainstorm the difficult ones and develop separate POA&Ms for those.

If you suspect not enough rigor has been applied to the project, ask about their brainstorming process. Use the TED method. "Tell me about…Explain…Describe". Use every project as an opportunity to mentor.

Even if the completion date for a task is months away, suggest your team begin work immediately. Ensure there are no expectations it will be acceptable to move completion dates to the right.

Choose a few of the distant tasks each week to investigate. "What did you do this week to satisfy this requirement?"

Note: Before leaving this chapter let's clarify information about other management / display tools. Use them. When there is one minor ripple in execution, project management software will show the impact quickly. The project manager will almost certainly be using one of the software tools. For reporting to or serving as the senior executive, use the tool that allows you to understand the activities and manage the tasks most effectively.

*Forrest Wayne Heard*

# Chapter 4

# Building a Learning Organization

As you are aware by this point, Robert L. Jackson set the conditions for building a learning organization. At the beginning of every project, he announced he was already thinking of the after-action review, the after-action report, and changes to be incorporated by the organization as a result of the learning. After a project was complete, he required his team to reflect on the life cycle of the project, and identify and debate observations about the planning and execution. In those discussions, he would encourage everyone to have thick skin.

Deming: **Learning is not compulsory…neither is survival.**

### Lessons Learned Activities Embedded in the Project Plan

In the task list for long-range projects, Jackson included meetings that were primarily devoted to gathering lessons learned. Jackson directed each member of his team to devote a section in their notebooks to gathering observations - things to improve, and good practices that needed to continue. They were primed to look for the good, the bad, and the ugly.

As the senior executive of the organization, Jackson developed a plan of action for incorporating the good ideas into the processes immediately. Unlike a common practice in many organizations, lessons did not walk out the door because of retirements, promotions, transfers, or poor memories. He ensured good ideas were captured, and changes made promptly. During the initial planning, he established suspense dates for making the changes suggested in the after-action review. He did not consider an operation (project) to be over, until all the 'fixes' and enhancements were in place.

As already noted, his occasional request of team members to share their observations during the progress report meetings heightened everyone's diligence in looking for improvements.

An officer who had served in the Republic of South Viet Nam as a young second lieutenant recounts how, upon arrival in Viet Nam, he was provided the unit's standing operating procedures (SOP). The SOP was a short document of policies and practices within the unit. He was directed to read it and pay attention to the good ideas, and the cautionary tales. He readily complied.

The SOP was a great source of sound advice, gleaned from years of hard-earned experience. It was prepared to keep him and his soldiers alive for the 12 months of their tours. After reading it, he was ready to go to work.

Thirty days later, he was tasked to write the unit's monthly lessons learned report. He had not understood the responsibility for submitting lessons learned rested upon each leader and those reports were due on a monthly basis. The monthly observations added to the growing list of good practices that were accumulating in the document he had read 30 days previously. He admitted anguishing over his first report. He had to dredge through every event he could remember to identify good and bad points about the month's operations.

However, he went on to say that after preparing the first report, the other eleven reports were relatively easy to write. The requirement to submit lessons learned prompted him to be on the lookout daily for areas of improvement. During the remainder of his time "in country", he was always looking for a better way, or shortcomings to correct. He developed the habit of looking for improvement opportunities. This acquired discipline proved useful later throughout his career in the corporate world.

How many of us are looking for areas of improvement every day as we go through our work?

Deming: **The aim of leadership is not merely to find and record failures of men, but to remove the causes of failure; to help people to do a better job with less effort**.

## Tips of the Trade

The leaders of the 5th Special Forces Group (SFG) were introduced to a world class lessons-learned program by a Special Forces legend, Master Sergeant (MSG) Joe C. Alderman.

The team leaders and team sergeants were summoned to the unit classroom. After settling into their seats, a very fit senior sergeant, the guest speaker, arrived carrying a stack of papers. Looking more like an IBM executive than combat veteran, MSG Alderman began their instruction.

Alderman distributed the packets that were approximately 20 pages in length. The title of the document was *Tips of the Trade - Lessons Learned by 5th SFG in Viet Nam.* The first page contained a list of things to do, and actions to avoid - Dos and Don'ts. The other 19 pages were the discussions that expounded on those recommendations. The pamphlet contained 'solid gold' for someone preparing for combat. Everyone who attended the meeting, or came across a copy during their careers, attested to the value of these 20 typed pages. It can be found on-line now.

These lessons were the result of the same system the lieutenant encountered when he arrived in Viet Nam. On a monthly basis, units engaged in the fight would identify lessons. *Tips of the Trade* was the end result. MSG Alderman had provided to these leaders, the next generation of Green Berets, a finished product; Jackson, on the other hand, showed his team how to start a program and gather the lessons.

## The After-Action Review

As already described, Jackson required everyone to be on the lookout for good ideas during a project or a field training exercise (war game).

One of the most effective meetings for observing and participating in an after-action review occurred in South Korea. Jackson's battalion had deployed from Hawaii to participate in an annual war game in the Republic of Korea. When his unit returned to the tent city after spending several days engaged in the war game, they began cleaning their gear for the return trip to Hawaii. As Jackson would routinely remind his unit, **"the training is not over until the equipment is ready to go to war again."** They had, of course, cleaned their weapons daily in the field but in a garrison environment one can do a much better job.

The company commanders (his direct reports) were summoned to headquarters. A map of the training area was posted on one wall, and a timeline of the exercise was recreated on another. Jackson set the stage for the review and transported everyone back to the first day of the operation. He reminded them of the missions each company had conducted, and they discussed from their notes what each had discovered in ways to improve.

They discussed each day, and every mission. Jackson probed the discussion to help the participants remember and uncover good practices and faulty assumptions. He pushed the conversation downward to help everyone focus on the minor details that, if neglected, could cripple a unit's capability to perform...like frostbite prevention.

At the end of an exhaustive discussion of the previous two weeks and all the team had discovered, and uncovered, he had built an impressive list of lessons learned. Before he adjourned the meeting, every lesson was discussed with respect to how the unit would correct or improve a faulty practice. Jackson established a suspense date for rewriting the unit's procedures. He insisted the scenario for the next field training at home station included the same situation that had triggered the suggestion. He wanted to ensure the recommendation was validated in practice and worked as well in the field as it had sounded in the debriefing room.

His actions from start to finish cemented the lessons into our business routines:

- Establish an expectation for an after-action review.

- Convene a meeting to record the observations immediately after an event, before memories fade and people depart through rotations to new assignments.

- Don't simply ask what was learned.

- Remind the attendees what happened from the beginning.

- Discuss key events and routine practices.

- Ask "how" one accomplished this task. "What was your response when... this event happened?"

Sometimes one must dig for the gold and treasure.

After the information was gathered, Jackson mandated actions that required the lessons to be implemented immediately and tested for validity.

- Draft the After-Action Report.

- Draft changes to the Unit SOP.

- Validate the changes in a tactical situation.

- Publish the AAR and updated SOP.

One of your last steps in managing a project is to convert the calendar dates to a D-day configuration. For example, if you undertook an initiative that had a due date of one year from start, D-365 represents the date you began. All the other dates are converted in relation to the due date—D-180…D-90…etc. Actions that happen after the completion of the project are D+days…D+30 may be the required date for publishing the new policy. This step is invaluable when confronted with the next project.

When tasked with a similar project, an initial review of the after-action report and D-day activities will provide insight into the schedule and potential bumps in the road. If the next due date shows a shorter suspense, the D-day list may reveal areas where you can tighten up the execution.

## Reflections on the Tips of the Trade

With current software, one could create a Dos and Don'ts page for every system at work in your organization and hyperlink the recommended action, or caution, to the discussion that predicated the lesson. Later, if pressed for time, you could take it on faith these are good ideas and should be followed. If you had ample time, you could read the "Federalist Paper" on that particular lesson.

### What other results can be produced from an After-Action Review?

Suppose, as you worked through your project, it became very apparent you really needed a gadget that could perform X function. Or you discovered you needed an employee with a special skill.

You might have uncovered the requirement for a special purchase or identified the need to hire someone else. Maybe you found your organization doesn't have a system that is needed, and you decide the best way to put a solution in place right now is to outsource the capability. Perhaps you need to find out who provides contracting and purchasing support in your organization, and then negotiate through the bureaucracy to make it happen. Or maybe, you're the decision maker and you want to look at several vendors.

## Implementing the Solution, Immediately

Sometimes, a solution can't wait. On one typically beautiful day in Hawaii, the company commanders (Jackson's leadership team) were engaged in training with their companies and received a radio call uncharacteristically summoning them to headquarters. Colonel Jackson wanted all the leaders to return to the headquarters, immediately. As already mentioned, Jackson was diligent in fencing everyone's time from unwarranted interruptions. Only something serious would necessitate pulling them from training.

As the team began to arrive, they were informed there had been a training accident on the grenade launcher range. A normal hand grenade is about the size of baseball, but heavier. Even the strongest person can only throw it so far. The grenade launcher, on the other hand, can propel a grenade a considerable distance. Unfortunately, if the barrel isn't elevated properly, the grenade can drop just a short distance in front of you, and explode. That occurred on this day.

No one was hurt, but an inspection of the weapon uncovered a problem with the sight. The grenade launcher sight consisted of a curved assembly that was graduated for ranges out to 400 meters. It had tooth-like gears. By manipulating a spring-loaded pin between the teeth, you could adjust the sight for the distance you estimated to your target.

The unit used a version of the sight made of a very durable plastic. Occasionally though, a tooth would break. This affected the sight in a very minor way. But, when several teeth were broken, it affected the aiming and trajectory of the grenade quite a bit more.

An inspection of the sight revealed several missing teeth. This caused the aiming point to slip, so the barrel wasn't elevated properly. Instead of going 150 meters toward the target, it only traveled about 20 meters before it impacted and exploded.

Jackson had a member of the staff research the inspection criteria of the grenade launcher sight and instruct the senior leaders of each company on the finer points of an inspection. He then released them with an admonishment to return to their units and check every sight for deficiencies. This after-action review and implementation of sound practices occurred immediately, before anyone went home for the day.

In a factory, you may be faced with a similar situation where a solution must be enacted immediately. And everyone who touches a particular piece of equipment is informed about proper procedures and the possibility of accident or injury.

## Root Cause Discovery

Something to consider: When the accident occurred, Jackson did not allow for a kneejerk response to determine why a round (term for a single bullet or grenade) exploded too close to the firing line. One might easily place blame on the shooter, or the sergeant who was providing safety oversight for the range.

Again, Jackson's mantra of **"Fix the problem, not the blame"** came through not just in word, but also in deed.

Jackson invested time to discover the real cause of the mishap. He took a similar approach to the unit's poor marksmanship results during the early days after taking the helm of the organization.

Jackson had implemented a more rigorous marksmanship program that should have increased everyone's scores - hits on targets. There was little improvement after the training.

He had observed the training and was confident the organization had implemented the latest information from the marksmanship training unit. Dry fire (trigger pull practice without bullets) indicated the soldiers should have increased their scores.

He arranged for a visit by a team from a higher-level maintenance organization. They were equipped with sophisticated inspection and measuring devices to evaluate the weapons, many of which were very old. This team had the capability to measure the deviations. They discovered that most of the barrels were bent and the bores (inside the barrel) were larger than normal. The barrels were out of tolerance. This caused a loss of energy and accuracy as the bullet wobbled down the barrel. The barrels were long past the end of their life cycles.

After replacing the barrels, Jackson's unit won five awards for expert marksmanship. Instead of placing blame on trainers or shooters, he looked for root causes and issues with the system.

Deming: "**A bad system will beat a good person every time**."

One final note about the grenade launcher incident

One of the first officers to arrive at headquarters observed Jackson handling this situation. One of the junior staff officers was phoning and placing radio calls to the commanders instructing them to come to the headquarters' building. The staff officer used the word 'emergency' in his conversation.

As he ended the call, Jackson corrected him.

## Suppress Panic by Providing Context

In typical fashion, Jackson asked, **"Is anyone bleeding?"** The answer was "No." **"Are there any units in a firefight and running low on ammunition?"** Again, "No, sir…"

**Jackson told the assembled group, "Those are the only two situations we consider emergencies. Everything else is just doing business."**

He helped his team understand how to define a real emergency and he squelched the tendency to panic or overreact. A real emergency for your operation should be defined. A fire may seem like a time to panic, unless you are in the fire department or on a ship. I heard one submariner express their value system when it comes to emergencies, **"All the solutions are down here."**

## Summarizing the Lessons Learned Program

- Establish the expectation.
- Plan for collection and implementation.
- Remind participants and collect routinely.
- Conduct the after-action review.
- Implement the changes.
- Validate the recommendations.

In Part I, you have looked at:

- How to analyze the requirements necessary to develop a solid plan of action;
- Considerations in managing the project - in the conference room and where the work actually happens; and

- Learning and improving along the way.

In Part II you will be introduced to a technique used by a singularly talented leader who transformed the culture and execution of a large complex organization through his personal action. His behavior spurred everyone to greater efforts and performance. You'll learn how to increase the knowledge, skills, and abilities of the workforce with a professional development program.

Your professional development program should ensure the employees, to include supervisors and managers, understand their responsibilities for maintaining the equipment.

You will observe how Jackson's organization developed a 24-month plan that included the major activities his organization would undertake.

You'll learn how leaders tie the systems together to develop synergy that supports your journey to excellence.

*Forrest Wayne Heard*

# Part II

These chapters will introduce or expand on the information that supports professional development of your organization (large or small). You'll be introduced to activities useful in developing the skills of the individual members in your office in managing projects, and other core skills necessary to succeed in the organization. These activities will facilitate developing and maintaining excellence throughout the corporation.

# Chapter 5

# Improving Self, Others, and Process Developing your Bench

There is no better way to improve the overall performance of your organization than through establishing a systematic, comprehensive professional development program. As a management consultant once told me, **"You hire qualified applicants, but you train good employees."**

Resumes and applications can tell you what employees should be able to do on the day they begin work. After they accept the position, one job of management is to ensure they understand the culture and values of the organization, along with internal policies and procedures. Another is to increase the knowledge, skills, and abilities of the workforce for the good of the organization, and for the improvement of the individual.

It is surprising to find some organizations are reluctant to provide employees with regular opportunities for training. In the Army, one could expect to spend the greater part of the first year of service in schools (education and training). Afterwards, on a cycle of about every three to four years, you attend a more advanced course in the system. These courses are part of the formal professional military education (PME) system. Units also sponsor local training and specialty courses for critical skills like the advanced medical training - Combat Life Saver. Even after selection to general officer, there are courses to attend and educational opportunities.

With some organizations there seems to be a fear of, or at least a reluctance to support training. Perhaps the cost to attend is a factor, or the employee's absence would impact the corporation in tangible and intangible ways. Managers might worry the employee could use the diploma or certification as a springboard to applying for a better paying job, with a competitor. The course might look attractive on the resume. A question sometimes asked is, **"What if I train them and they leave?"** A better question to ask may be **"What if you don't train them, and they stay?"**

Of course, there are some companies famous for their training programs, the commitment of top management to those programs, and their renown for having a competitive edge in the market.

Some units in DoD habitually take the long view. As soon as young soldiers with leadership potential were identified, or earned sergeant stripes, some organizations began lining up schools that prepared them to serve in positions of greater responsibility and supported their career progression.

One highly anticipated course in airborne (paratrooper) units qualified a new sergeant to serve as a jumpmaster for an airborne operation. As jumpmaster, the NCO was responsible for briefing 60+ jumpers, several of whom might be senior leaders in the organization; inspecting each jumper to ensure the equipment was rigged properly; and controlling the actions at the door as the jumpers exited. Units that took the long view invariably had plenty of qualified jumpmasters for their operations.

On the other hand, other organizations were constantly plagued by shortages in qualified personnel in critical positions, like jumpmasters. Whenever there were school allocations—available seats in a course—their shortsighted response was often, "We can't afford to release anyone for the class, at this time. We have 'X event' coming up and we'll need all our leaders there." It took the personal intervention of a new senior executive—COL Stang—to adjust the mindset, change the culture, and encourage the leaders to adopt the long view.

Jim Collins, in his bestseller *Good to Great,* advises a company must **get the right people on the bus and in the right seats and the wrong people off the bus.** In some cases, the bus is loaded before it arrives at your stop. When you step on board, you will be looking at the team that is already assembled. You may be able to affect the seating arrangements in the short term, and influence who is riding on your bus in the long run, but initially you will probably go with the current busload. The longer you are in place or the greater your authority, the closer you can follow Collins's great advice. With the right people on your bus, the wrong people off, regardless of bumps in the road—curveballs thrown by the competition, market, and global politics—your organization will have the best chances for survival.

In the military, one generally accepts the busload that is provided. Of course, provisions are in place to remove someone from the bus if they are consistently poor performers.

An internal professional development program allows you to upgrade the knowledge of everyone on your bus; focus the training on key skills and abilities you, as the senior executive, along with your leadership team, identify as supporting the core competencies of your organization; and shore up the areas where you have identified opportunities for improvement.

Other than funding, another concern of managers involves the time away from the office or the production line, i.e. not being engaged in the activities that generate income. How might their absence adversely impact the bottom line?

A large mutual life insurance company has designed a robust preparation program for the agents in their initial three years with the company. The associate (their title for agent) undergoes several weeks of training before being allowed out onto the streets to represent the company. After this basic course, their apprenticeship is far from over. The company trainers provide structured weekly, then monthly, and finally quarterly instruction to novice associates.

Furthermore, the agents are strongly encouraged to participate in courses sponsored by the financial services industry to gain additional knowledge, and certifications.

After becoming competent associates and serving in their second year, agents are still routinely pulled out of production to attend more training. What is the impact of not calling for appointments or pounding the streets during those numerous training days? This company has led the Million Dollar Round Table—the gold standard for insurance production—for years, although it doesn't field the largest sales force. It would appear this company has seen a correlation in training and production.

## Individual Development

Jackson established a professional development program, which ensured his senior leaders refined the skills he understood to be important for managing large, complex organizations. He also arranged for the midlevel managers to receive similar education and training. Even those who were being considered for promotion to first-line supervisors attended routine, structured, professional development training.

In Army organizations, there are officers, noncommissioned officers (NCOs), and junior enlisted. Jackson managed the professional development program for the officers. He directed his senior enlisted soldier, the Command Sergeant Major (CSM), to develop a similar one for the NCOs. The CSM charged the First Sergeants (1SGs), who are the senior enlisted members in each company, with the responsibility to identify the junior enlisted soldiers displaying NCO potential, and craft a program to help prepare them for positions of greater responsibility.

There are organizations claiming to have a professional development program, because they occasionally entertain a guest speaker, or call an ad hoc assembly to talk about a current event, changes mandated by Congress, or other topical subjects. These unscheduled opportunity meetings wouldn't qualify as a Jackson-style professional development program.

Jackson's professional development program was the result of task analysis focused on determining what skills officers would need to hone to excellence for their current duties; the additional skills needed as they moved on to more demanding positions; and the common skills, which, in most organizations, were not addressed. All the interrelated systems within the organization were subjects for training - administration, maintenance, training, readiness, retention, logistics, etc.

Drucker: **We now accept the fact that learning is a lifelong process of keeping abreast of change. And the most pressing task is to teach people how to learn.**

Remarkably, a list of the majority of tasks that factored into the professional development program had been available during the offsite at which they had initially met to develop the 24-month training program. Jackson had already considered the additional training he wanted the officers to undergo and prepared the list for scheduling. But that's not all (as the TV announcer might say), he also required the property book officer to prepare a list of every piece of hardware —large or small— used by the battalion.

When the officers met to develop the long-range calendar, they consulted both lists as they prepared each week of the next 24 months. The company commanders selected professional development topics and identified pieces of equipment on which they would focus the organization's attention. Did this schedule sometimes change; did they sometimes switch to a different piece of equipment? Of course! **"Audibles are always allowed, but we have to know how to line up at the scrimmage."**

When the organization experienced the grenade range incident (see Chapter 4), the unit adjusted and substituted the grenade launcher and ancillary equipment as the focus of training and maintenance for that week. A vehicle had originally been scheduled as the subject of maintenance training. The vehicle was not forgotten, though. The leaders doubled up the maintenance training a few weeks later and brought the published schedule back in line.

By selecting the topic, and scheduling the date and instructor during the offsite, Jackson allowed maximum preparation time for ensuring excellent training, and innovative delivery of information. Delivery of high-quality instruction became a competition among his company commanders. Everyone benefited. The program resulted in positive, constructive, healthy competition among the commanders.

As one moves up in your corporation, performing the factory floor tasks may not be an effective use of fenced time for professional development. That doesn't mean the training should end.

Subject matter experts (SMEs) within your own organization can be called upon to provide insights into their internal processes or how they interact with corporate headquarters. If you are in production management, maybe your shortcoming involves financial statements and how your performance affects them. You need information from the finance team to round out your talent and upgrade your own skills. Perhaps you are in marketing, and you need to understand the production management process to increase your long-term potential. There are endless courses on-line or that can be ordered to polish your skills in critical decision making, transformational leadership, lean manufacturing, etc.

Perhaps you haven't served as the project manager for a complex project, so you are assigned a project to help get your legs under you.

Jackson served as group mentor to all officers in the organization through his professional development program. He personally mentored everyone who reported directly to him. Furthermore, by establishing a program and rhythm, and a focus on continuous improvement, he educated his team about organizing professional development programs in their future assignments.

Professor Roberto, in the Great Courses Lesson on Critical Decision Making made this comment about case studies at the Harvard's summer camp for professors: "**How we learn is what we learn.**" Jackson ensured younger officers would understand professional development to be a natural part of managing a large organization, and how to install an effective program when they became senior leaders of organizations.

## Mentor

Mentor, of course, conjures up the whole story of The Trojan War. Odysseus, King of Ithaca, craftiest of the Greek kings, realized that while he was away, his young son, Telemachus, would need instruction in the skills of a warrior, and wisdom to rule. Before he left to fight the war in Troy, Odysseus asked his friend, Mentor, to tutor the prince. Mentor's name became synonymous with someone who guides and coaches another, usually junior, in critical skills. Some organizations are using younger employees to mentor the older, less tech-savvy, senior personnel.

As with every project Jackson undertook, he understood the importance of personal attention and attendance. He was adamant everyone in management (the officers of the organization) attend the training. He considered it vital to their development and long-term value to the larger organization.

At the beginning of each class, he would casually ask each of the company commanders if all their officers were present. Woe betide those who allowed one of their officers to skip the training to perform something they considered more important. To Jackson, nothing was more important in peace time than improving oneself. He was not at all reluctant in directing the commander to place a call to the errant officer. Every leader's place of duty was at the session. Jackson was always unambiguous about the requirement to attend *his training program*.

## Classroom

The education and training program for leaders took many forms. Often, all the officers of the organization would meet in a conference room for a class. Jackson would occasionally deliver the training himself. He might discuss ethics and applications in ambiguous situations, or common denominators for those selected for promotion during recent national level promotion boards. On other occasions, one of the specialty staff members might provide insights into esoteric programs, which needed our attention.

## Field craft and Tactics

For other sessions, the officers would assemble in tactical training areas (the woods) and participate in advanced instruction on tactics or weapons systems.

## Maintenance Training

One additional half-hour (or sometimes an hour) each week was devoted to learning about the organizational equipment—how to employ and maintain every piece of hardware the unit wore, carried, rode, or used. The piece of equipment serving as the focus for the week was selected from the list, at the offsite. Each of Jackson's senior subordinates—the company commanders—would learn how to spot-check and troubleshoot the item, and conduct immediate action to put the piece of equipment back into operation when it stopped working. We addressed the inspection and maintenance of the grenade launcher and the sights during one of these half-hour sessions.

The leaders were expected to return to their organizations and provide the same inspection, maintenance, and troubleshooting information to their teams. It was a weekly train-the-trainer program. During any twelve months, the leaders examined every piece of equipment belonging to the organization, increasing their expertise in employing and maintaining each piece of gear.

It requires no stretch of the imagination to understand how this routine would support the work of an assembly plant, warehouse, or tool and die operation.

At Jackson's weekly workshops, the company commanders were the trainers. It has been said no one learns better than those who prepare and provide the training.

Consider this: If you teach a subject five times, each group of attendees hears it once. You hear it five times. In responding to questions, you must think about the situations presented in the discussion. In addition, it may take 8 hours of preparation for each hour you are training others.

Using your most junior employees to teach other members of your office is a great way to develop them, professionally. It has been my experience that engagement in meaningful activity (teaching others) increases job satisfaction.

## Team Training

In the Army, and in the factory on a production line, there are many activities that are accomplished by the efforts of teams. You have already examined Florer's technique for upgrading the performance of his core staff. Jackson added another piece to the professional development puzzle. Jackson used Model Unit Training (MUT) to establish a high standard of performance in team activities. MUT ensures everyone in the organization participating in a specific team activity is exposed to the 'best practices' for that activity, the benchmark.

As an example: One of the group skills that bedeviled mortar platoons in tactical assessments and evaluations was occupying a position at night. This might sound fairly easy, but it's not. It required a stealthy reconnaissance, bringing the mortars forward, establishing wire communications (telephones) within the position, and ensuring the guns were located with pinpoint accuracy, pointed in the right direction, and precisely parallel. Firing a mortar that is even slightly askew can result in a high explosive round impacting among friendly personnel. A slight error at the gun position results in a large error down range.

All the activities involved in occupation of the night firing position were carried out without a light source. The tasks could prove difficult. The occupation was evaluated against the clock. Very little time was allowed after moving into the area before the guns had to be ready to fire. Performance could range from sloppy execution that was fast, in one quadrant, to meticulously correct occupation that was slow, in another. Both extremes resulted in failure. There was no tolerance when measuring the accuracy or speed of execution. The time difference between passing, and failing, was one second. The platoon either completed within the time allowed, or did not.

In preparation for the MUT, one mortar platoon (approximately 20 personnel) was tasked to brainstorm the drill to determine where a few minutes or even seconds could be shaved from each step. The platoon tested the suggestions and adopted solutions. When the platoon proved they were able to meet the requirements, consistently, they demonstrated the drill to all mortar platoons, discussing tips that worked and those that were suggested but did not work under field conditions.

Senior mortarmen, who attended the training, suggested additional tips to save time, and generally played Devil's Advocates. The process and the procedures of occupying a position at night became standardized throughout the organization. The tips were produced in a Best Practices document for inclusion in unit SOPs. MUT was just one of the ways Jackson increased the performance levels of every team.

As you ponder this program and Jackson's approach, consider this: Every year, under Jackson's leadership, his leaders conducted approximately:

- 52 focused training events highlighting the inspection and maintenance of a specific piece equipment, followed by the systematic maintenance of those items,

- 24 (two-hour) professional development sessions, focusing on tactics and leadership knowledge and skills, and

- Several (usually one per month) Model Unit Training opportunities.

Consider how much more effective your team could be by instituting and supporting a similar professional development program in your organization.

Imagine your focus is production management. Are there processes you would like improved? How would the ability to quickly change dies and switch to a different product impact your bottom line? How are you going about increasing the individual skills (management, along with rank and file) and team performance? Do you have a program?

If Jackson asked a leader if they are going to meet their training or maintenance objectives and one replied with, "I hope so." Jackson was fond of saying, "**Hope is not a means**." What is your plan?

## Developing Your Bench Strength

A concept long used by Green Beret organizations is cross-training. This technique increases the skills of your team members and the capability of your team.

Cross-training is a technique for building the bench strength within your organization by ensuring everyone knows the jobs of at least one other. Green Beret detachments often worked in a split team concept. This required identical skills replicated in both teams. In each half, there was one expert in each specialty—communications, medical, and weapons.

The leaders on the team ensured every member of the team knew the basic skills of all these specialties. If your weapons man can administer an IV (intravenous therapy) to a soldier with a minor wound, your medic can solve some of the more serious problems in triage. Cross-training was even more important when the team member who possessed deep knowledge and experience, is wounded, or worse. Someone must assume his duties. Green Berets manage to build a deep bench through cross training.

Often, specialty training on medical issues would be delivered by the weapons specialist under the guidance of the medic. Struggling to prepare a class outside of your specific expertise increases your skills exponentially. This proved more effective in developing a soldier's skills than relying on the medic teaching medical tasks, communicators teaching antenna theory, and the weapons leader showing how to put a foreign manufactured machine gun into action.

The more mature teams would require the training to be delivered in the language of the target country, adding another layer of difficulty.

Jackson's improvement programs were directly focused on making the incremental improvements in the organization's processes. If you study lean manufacturing, you'll see a corollary to his techniques. In conference with his direct reports, Jackson might ask, "How could we do this better, or faster, with fewer resources?"

### Managing the Personal Development of Your Team

Jackson's improvement program took many forms but three such programs are highlighted here.

### Performance Counseling and Evaluations

### The Annual Plan

In the first week of an assignment to Jackson's organization, he met with the newly assigned officer in a formal setting. He would ask the officer to prepare a list of objectives for the upcoming year for this opening discussion. Jackson reviewed the list, asking probing questions. Before adjourning, he might ask the officer to move a few items higher on the list. Fitness and marksmanship were two very important values on which he wanted every leader's commitment. For every objective, he asked the officer to add the phrase - *as indicated by* - and then complete the sentence before returning for next month's counseling.

Where the officer had written, 'increase the physical conditioning of the company' on his list, Jackson wanted him to identify the measurement by which they would know when success was achieved - an objective measurement. A generally stated fitness objective became, "Increase the physical conditioning of the company *as indicated by* qualifying for and retaining the Silver Streamer award. (The Silver Streamer was a program sponsored by the division headquarters that evaluated the physical fitness of units. Prior to Jackson assuming command, the success rate for earning the Silver Streamer was low. An outside agency conducted the testing. Very soon after Jackson's arrival, all five companies in his battalion qualified for the Silver Streamer.)

## Mess or Dining Facility Officer

The objective assigned to the dining facility officer was certainly a big, hairy audacious goal. Jackson considered food part of the soldier's pay. If, in the hometown recruiting efforts, young people were told they'd be paid a salary plus fed and housed, then he expected the food to be well prepared and the barracks (living quarters) properly maintained. The advertised perquisite (perq) needed to meet expectations. He was a big proponent of truth in advertising.

He directed the mess officer to list as one of his objectives, "We will provide a high-quality dining experience in the mess hall *as indicated by* earning the national award for mess halls." This was an incredible stretch goal. The dining facility, in fact, won the Connelly award presented to mess halls at the national level competition.

When the team returned from the awards ceremony, the mess officer was justifiably proud of their accomplishments. Jackson was proud of their efforts, too. But to ensure no one rested on their laurels, Jackson asked the mess officer to change his primary objective for the next year to "We will provide high quality food *in the field*, as indicated by…

The next year, the mess team competed in the category of field mess.

Units employ field mess equipment when in combat or during sustained field operations. Field kitchens and mess kit laundries are established. For the Connelly Award, in the field mess category, the organization is evaluated not only in quality of food, but also in tactical prowess. Again, the team competed at the national level. Food was part of the soldier's pay.

Jackson's simple goal for his organization was excellence in all they did.

## Monthly Follow-up

Jackson's method for mentoring you individually included monthly follow-up meetings about your performance plan. In these one-on-one counseling sessions, you reviewed the list of objectives and progress. If he had observed something he felt was your greatest weakness, or your weakest strength, in relation to others working at the same level, he would identify it.

Unlike many supervisors, Jackson would help you identify those areas that prevented you from being best in show. If he thought your physical condition was not the best among the ones you would be evaluated against, he would let you know. If administration of your organization was your weak spot, you would hear it from him in one of these sessions. He used the sessions to help you improve, to coach you. When it came time for annual appraisals, you always knew where you stood. There were no surprises.

Some managers seem to counsel subordinates regarding performance, only when there is an unsatisfactory situation to address, or it is time for an annual performance review. They rarely provide feedback until annual appraisal time. On the other hand, Jackson's almost continuous dialog created a strong bond between himself and his leadership team.

Another story of personal counseling concerns a life insurance company and Steve Adkins, the managing partner of the local office in Charleston, South Carolina. Steve would spend time, each week advising new associates. After a few sessions, he'd turn the tables around, asking, "If I was the new agent, what advice would you me give on increasing my sales?" After you stumbled through a few suggestions and exhausted your advice, he would ask, "Is it okay if I add a few ideas that worked for me when I was an agent?" He would then provide excellent advice based on his experience.

This is an effective technique designed to increase performance. It spurs a deeper level of thought than required by sitting passively and listening to advice…even good advice.

## Personal Instruction in Organizing, Planning, and Executing Training and Operations

The third category of personal engagement Jackson employed to hone one's skills were the once-a-week production plan, or training schedule, meetings.

The ability to develop long-range, detailed plans of complex and coordinated activities is a critical and highly valued skill among military organizations. Jackson's meetings included a line-by-line scrutiny of everything you had planned and coordinated. The plans were developed and discussed with Jackson four to six weeks in advance. Until he had fine-tuned your planning skills and felt satisfied with your level of competence, the meetings were a crucible. The significantly productive process he developed and implemented was unlike any training schedule approval procedure I had seen in use in other highly respected organizations, in DoD.

Due to his personal attention in developing this skill in his commanders, they became highly capable in analyzing competencies and opportunities. They became efficient in crafting plans to upgrade the abilities of individuals and teams and coordinating the necessary support (some with long lead times) for the activities in the plan, be it transportation, aircraft, ammunition, or training areas.

Jackson's commanders learned to forecast requirements 18 to 24 months into the future and manage a training program that would build on lessons and activities, linking preceding weeks, taking into account personnel turnover, and resources. Other senior leaders in the division would often recruit from this battalion for operations, training, and readiness officers (called S3s in the Army).

## Summary

The formal methods Jackson used for developing the knowledge and skills of his team included

- The professional development program.

- The maintenance training program.

- The individual performance counseling.

- The individual training schedule discussions.

- His project management and meeting disciplines.

These were the formal methods by which he passed along the skills needed to serve at higher echelons of the Army.

His informal, but just as important, technique included routine visits and conversations about your organization and your aspirations. Using the Socratic method of questioning, he helped you discover things about the organization and managing the many systems involved, along with employing your teams effectively.

Once, in response to a question, Jackson provided a 15-minute impromptu class to his commanders and staff about coordinating and conducting an air assault (helicopter) operation to seize an objective in enemy held territory. His off-the-cuff instruction included critical information that was never discussed at Fort Benning's Infantry courses, the U.S. Army Ranger School, or Special Forces Officer Course. Not only had these tips never made it to the classrooms, these long-forgotten, except to Jackson, insights weren't recorded in any of the doctrinal manuals (How-to books). His experience, common sense, and brilliance changed how the organization prepared and operated helicopter assaults from that day forward.

Of course, the organization immediately changed their standing operating procedures (SOP) for air assault operations, incorporating these insights.

Jackson would routinely discuss a military event in history that showed how enforcing a good practice prevented disaster or how neglecting a policy or tactic resulted in soldiers dying. He helped you learn from the mistakes, or good practices of others who had gone before us. Jackson never told heroic war stories that put himself at the center of attention. His personal stories were mostly humorous or revealed a misstep on his part, which shaped his belief system. Jackson, like the others in this book, was humble but demanding. He was a Level 5 Leader, to use Collins's term. (Collins also coined the term "big hairy audacious goal").

One of the guiding principles in uniformed service is you must train your replacement. You must engage the professional development concept from the perspective 'if I get hit by a truck on the way to work today what does my team and my deputy need to know?' Another sobering thought is not everyone who starts out to take the objective will live to reach the top of the hill. You must build bench strength in your leadership pool, redundancy in your critical skills, and prepare others to take your place.

Angela Ahrendt: "**I believe succession planning is one of the greatest responsibilities you have as a leader. So when your time comes to move on, your team not only doesn't**

**miss a beat but gains in momentum, embracing new challenges and realizing future opportunities**.

In the next chapter you will take a deeper dive in the work of increasing the skills in keeping your equipment operating at maximum effectiveness. And be entertained by a glimpse into the story of how one platoon of college Reserve Officer Training Corps (ROTC) cadets learned an invaluable lesson about the serious business of supervising the maintenance of vehicles.

*Forrest Wayne Heard*

# Chapter 6

# Husband the Resources
# Taking care of the Equipment

One area where Bob Jackson focused his considerable knowledge and energies was ensuring the equipment of the organization remained in top readiness (ready-to-go-to-war) posture. He routinely reminded his leadership team of their obligations to the taxpayers, and the wisdom of ensuring every piece of gear carried to war worked when it was needed.

In plant operations, you should have the same concern for keeping the equipment in topnotch condition.

As a war game ended, he would enjoin the leaders with **"the training isn't over, until the equipment is ready to go to war again."** He emphasized, and applied his energies to, maintenance with the same enthusiasm that most leaders reserved for training. He acted more like a business owner who had personally purchased the equipment than a casual caretaker. Jackson expected (demanded) the same from his team.

Taking care of the equipment was always a subject of high interest within the Army, but never was the policy, and value, reflected in such tangible behavior as with Jackson. His determination to train his officers, and expand their general understanding of the Army's maintenance system into a comprehensive and detailed body of knowledge was unsurpassed. In doing so, he increased the maintenance posture to an unrivaled level.

There is a story of General Patton, of WWII fame, asking a tanker how far the vehicle would travel with a full load of fuel. The crewmen answered with the exact information contained in the technical manual. Patton replied he didn't mean what was the average according to the manual, he meant *this tank*. Patton wanted to ensure crewmen knew how much fuel that particular tank used when on the march, or in a fight. Jackson used that same logic. Make it personal.

## Spare Parts Management

This story might give you an idea of how deep Jackson's interest and expectations lay. For each piece of equipment the Army uses, there is a prescribed load list (PLL). This is the overarching name for the spare parts that must be kept on the shelf in the repair facility for repairs due to normal wear and tear. The PLL was, no doubt, developed by the combined genius of equipment designers, engineers, experts, mechanics, and test team to set the conditions for a well-supplied garage, weapons room, or communications facility. PLL is a little understood program that receives only a small amount of attention during the professional military education system.

Most personnel believe the PLL reflects what should be on the shelf, and the parts accurately reflect what the unit would need on-hand, to keep their weapons, radios, and vehicles in perfect working order. Jackson turned that world upside down.

Bob Jackson required his company commanders to monitor the actual usage of parts (those off-the-shelf and those that had to be ordered) to keep the equipment operating. After every major field exercise or extended marksmanship event, the commanders recorded and reported their parts usage. Jackson arranged one of the weekly maintenance classes to instruct his direct reports in the Army's (little known) process for adjusting the PLL (It ceased being a sacrosanct parts list developed by unseen, long-forgotten geniuses).

Instead of continuing the practice of stocking shelves based on guidelines developed when the equipment was originally fielded, his organization began using actual results. By requiring the adjustment after every training event and inserting the requirement to confront actual usage into his unit policies and SOP, the activity was not a one-time event. Review and adjustment became part of the way we did business.

This practice resulted in more accurate stocking of the shelves; fewer parts ordered using the emergency requisition system, and less waste. Waste can occur when parts that aren't needed sit on shelves until obsolete; losses through packing and unloading inherent in field maintenance activities; and general inattention.

When challenged and contradicted by local experts in the higher-level maintenance organization, they were referred to regulations governing their operations, along with the change process for PLL. Officers under Jackson were no longer just good officers and managers; he required them to work at a much higher, professional level. He conscientiously challenged the conventional wisdom. Like the citizens of Missouri, he demanded of the experts, "Show me."

Without a manager like Jackson, requiring research (into a process he was already cognizant of) and study, no one would have stumbled across this information. The regulations were not part of the common body of knowledge, or casual reading, for those outside of the maintenance field. Nor was it, in fact, common knowledge by members of those inside the maintenance management organizations.

This situation and encounter with the purported experts are reflected in the story of General Meloy's meeting with the assignments and administrative experts. He schooled them on the technical aspects of their own regulations. Meloy's story, in Chapter 7, is the centerpiece of the discussion on transformation of large, complex organizations.

Having touched on certain aspects of the maintenance practices in Jackson's organization, more details of the program will now be explained. This section will provide ideas in establishing a maintenance management and training program in your organization.

## Scheduling the Maintenance Area of Focus

In Chapter 5, you were introduced to the setup for the long-range planning meeting. At the offsite, there was a 24-month timeline depicted on a roll of paper that surrounded the room. On this calendar, the officers began scheduling the maintenance activities, aligned with the training schedule.

By using paper, versus computer projections, Jackson's team could see, and use, all 24 months with ease, without scrolling a computer screen. One company commander could be working on the activities of May of the upcoming year, while another was working on August of the current year. As a commander read the work of another commander it sparked ideas for their own training plan. After the week of projecting training, maintenance, and professional development education activities, this 24-month calendar prepared on the roll of paper was referred to as the *scroll*.

In Chapter 9, there will be a more comprehensive discussion of the long-range planning technique. Any loose ends regarding how this 24-month plan was prepared and used will be tied up in Chapter 9. Using this method for projecting, planning, and scheduling is a very effective technique. It allows for visualizing and aligning your intent and activities to fulfill your organizational goals.

Through experience, the officers knew that certain items of equipment would receive more usage when the unit was involved in extended field training. During the weeks leading up deployment they would schedule instruction, followed by the inspections and maintenance, on those specialty items used in a field environment, such as large tents, space heaters, kitchen equipment, etc.

If, on the other hand, the unit planned to be engaged in marksmanship training and live-fire exercises, the leaders focused their efforts on maintenance of weapons and ancillary equipment during the weeks preceding these training events.

Some equipment seemed to receive a constant amount of use irrespective of the training focus. Those items were selected to fill in the gaps in the schedule.

As his officers determined what equipment made sense for education and maintenance for that week, the responsibility for training rotated among the company commanders. Eventually, even the most neglected piece of hardware was subjected to the rigorous instruction, and maintenance process. Nothing on the shelves, in the motor pools, arms rooms, or supply rooms, was deemed too trivial. Within 12 months, everything the battalion rode, carried, wore, and used had received concentrated attention - both in education about the equipment and actual maintenance of the gear. Maintenance happened daily. Focused maintenance training occurred weekly.

## Reviewing the Status, Managing the Maintenance

Every Friday, his leadership team—the commanders and the battalion staff—reviewed the condition of every item in the inventory during a one-hour maintenance meeting. The discussion focused on equipment that was broken (inoperable) and expected repair date. If awaiting a part, you were expected to be conversant in the location of that part as it traveled the supply chain. If the part arrived and was now on the shelf, there was an expectation that no one would leave work until the vehicle was ready to roll, the weapon ready to fire, or the radio was in good working order.

Why was this so important?

Had the unit been notified, in the middle of the night, that a situation had developed and the organization was to be committed immediately, for combat, the deployment would not be delayed for a repair that could have (should have) been completed the day before.

Along with the status of equipment and unit maintenance activities, the maintenance officer also identified those items that were due for higher level maintenance. This weekly update afforded Jackson's leaders awareness of the availability of the equipment and when it would be unavailable for use. In the case of a vehicle, it allowed time for Jackson's commanders to make other arrangements for transportation. This system also supported the maintenance supervisor's planning for garage space and mechanics.

## Managing the Expendable Supplies

Jackson's idea of maintaining the organization wasn't limited to end items - major pieces of equipment. During the maintenance review, he required information on the unit's stock of batteries and other expendables. These were reported by number of days on hand, such as a 30, 60, or 90-day supply.

## Managing the Personnel Actions

Not one to engage in half measures, he required the human resource office to monitor personnel replacements, and departures—managing the maintenance of personnel assignments. His 30, 60, 90-day list of those personnel moving within the unit or scheduled to transfer to their next assignments helped him manage end-of-tour performance reports and awards. Tracking transfers afforded everyone ample time to prepare the documentation resulting in evaluations that were not rushed, eliminating comments that appeared to be afterthoughts.

Remaining aware of losses enabled him to gauge the appropriate lead time to groom someone to replace a key loss to the organization and when to throttle back on tasks being assigned to a departing soldier. Transfers include substantial out-processing requirements, to include packing the family's household goods for yet another move.

## Managing Attendance at Corporate-run Schools

Each month, Jackson would convene a special meeting to 'maintain and manage' the training of the junior NCOs. He managed the order of merit list (the attendance list) for NCO advancement and development schools. In one meeting, an officer suggested one of his very competent young NCOs would be needed during the upcoming training exercise.

He recommended the NCO not attend the course that conflicted with those dates. Jackson suggested, with a smile, the same treatment for this officer.

He asked the young officer how it would affect his own career if Jackson notified Army headquarters not to select this officer for any additional advanced schooling because he was too valuable to the unit. (Of course, a comment like that on a performance evaluation would, without a doubt, end an officer's career.)

The young commander, and all those in attendance, understood his point. Jackson always took the long view regardless of the short-term pain of operating without a key leader. He wanted his subordinate leaders to adopt that same foresight for the good of the local unit, but also for the good it would do for the Army as a whole, in the future.

Like the other areas where Jackson applied his talents, he did not limit his management activities to the status meetings every Friday. It was no surprise to receive a hushed phone call informing you the battalion commander was in the motor pool, or the arms room. "He's looking at the equipment and the paperwork!" By patterning themselves after Jackson, his commanders became better managers and maintainers.

Louis V. Gerstner, Jr. **"I have always believed you cannot run a successful enterprise from behind a desk."**

## Maintenance Training

As previously reported, Jackson considered maintenance training to be just as important as other, more exciting, training, like dropping mortar rounds, or calling in aircraft for a strafing run. (Maybe not as important, but important, nonetheless.)

Immediately after the Friday maintenance meeting, the commanders and staff adjourned to a site outside and began maintenance training. The company commander, who selected this piece of gear months ago, would have prepared a packet of notes for each of the attendees. He would provide general information about the piece of equipment; cite the references; provide the checklist for daily inspections (before, during, and after use); along with other pertinent information developed through experience and by researching all pertinent maintenance publications.

The instructor would talk through a spot check and identify some of the key problem areas and how to remedy them (troubleshooting). In addition, he had to be prepared to respond to Jackson's sure-to-be-asked questions.

After this class (30 minutes to an hour), the commanders returned to their respective companies and reviewed the information with their leadership teams—the lieutenants and sergeants.

Mondays and Fridays were generally devoted to focused maintenance and administrative activities. The item of equipment on which they were to train was already on the schedule as the focus of detailed inspection, and comprehensive maintenance during that Friday afternoon, or on the upcoming Monday.

## An Ethics Note

Very early, and often, during Jackson's tenure as the senior executive of the organization he ensured every leader fully understood the correct way for maintaining a 100% operational ready rate on equipment. The approved manner was limited to the official maintenance system. The unapproved technique that has been commonly used in some outfits was to allow one of your junior personnel to pilfer parts from a sister unit. Have a parts problem? Call for the scrounger. (Jim Hutton's role as SGT Peterson, in *The Green Berets*, was introduced as he was caught scrounging for another Special Forces Group.)

Jackson made it abundantly clear that stealing from another unit was totally unacceptable and he would deal with the situation and the commanders harshly. It was the company commanders' duty to ensure everyone in their company - mechanics, supervisors, and other well-meaning competitive employees - understood this activity would not be tolerated. He recommended whenever leaders addressed their maintenance teams, they return to the ethics theme often to ensure it soaked in. Jackson knew it was necessary for all recent arrivals to hear it directly from a company commander, early in their assignments with this unit.

Bob Jackson instructed his leaders on what he referred to as constructive and destructive competition, or healthy and unhealthy competition. (One aspect of healthy competition was already mentioned as his commanders delivered training to fellow officers.) Jackson was a huge supporter of healthy, constructive, positive competition. He encouraged healthy competition. He warned of buying into competition without a heavy dose of ethics. He counseled his leadership team to understand in combat they will be depending on the sister battalions to the left and right of them. They were only to engage in healthy competition and compete in a constructive manner.

In communicating important information—values, safety, and beliefs—it's important to say it early and often to ensure everyone in your organization hears it from you. Certain information needs to be like a Broadway production. Remember, even though you are saying the same things over and over, the audience is new. **Let us not grow tired of doing good, for in due time we shall reap our harvest, if we do not give up. (Galatians 6:9)**

Or, as Winston S. Churchill explained to the Prince of Wales, future King Edward VIII: **"If you have an important point to make, don't try to be subtle or clever. Use a pile driver. Hit the point once. Then come back and hit it again. Then hit it a third time – a tremendous whack."**

Your key points need to be talked about in the executive suite and on the shop floor, offices, loading docks and all points in between. In addition, the values and behaviors need to be lived in front of the organization.

## Daily Preventive Maintenance Checks and Services (PMCS)

In an earlier chapter, you may remember METT-TC was compared to PMCS…**always endorsed, rarely enforced.**

Jackson imposed a set of checks and balances to ensure drivers and supervisors were trained, and no vehicles rolled out of the motor pool gate without undergoing PMCS. When the vehicles were returned at the end of the duty day, they were also inspected and prepared for the next day's labor. (The day wasn't over until the equipment was ready to go to war again.)

All drivers were trained and complied with policy. Policy became practice.

An old horse cavalry practice required the soldier to take care of the horse before taking care of himself. This concern was carried over in an established standard for vehicles (when they replaced horses), weapons, and other equipment.

Blending maintenance training along with the maintenance activities increased everyone's knowledge, skills, and abilities in maintaining the gear, and resulted in improving the maintenance posture of every piece of equipment. It was a highlight of Jackson's management program.

There were many organizations throughout the Army that took maintenance seriously. The senior executives of those units ensured the organization and equipment was ready to go to war. Their maintenance programs were, no doubt, similar to Jackson's.

Unfortunately, in other organizations, the reality was often, significantly, different. The term PMCS has always enjoyed widespread use but not widespread understanding. To some, PMCS meant to check the oil, and other fluid levels before driving. To others, it might include a check of fluid levels plus lights and horn. To a few it meant a full inspection using the checklist from the technical manual: before operating the equipment; during use; and at the end of the day. This is true PMCS.

This disparity in understanding can be exposed very quickly with a few of those annoying follow-on questions that help peel back the onion. As a plant manager or supervisor, you can find out the ground truth (reality) easily by adopting this habit.

After asking an operator if the maintenance has been completed, and receiving a positive reply, a conversation might develop along these lines: "Great! Could you walk me through the process?"

Response: "What do you mean?"

Inspector: "Well, what technical manual (TM) did you use? Where is your TM? Do you have a copy of the checklist? How did you go about ensuring the lights and turn signals worked? (Look for an action that must be supported by an assistant.) Who assisted you on that? When you checked on …name an item…what were you looking for? What situation should cause you concern or deadline the vehicle? How fast should you be going when you apply pressure to the brakes to see if the vehicle pulls to the left or right?"

There are a number of informed questions to ask to evaluate a person's knowledge about inspecting and operating equipment. One generally does not have to dig very deeply to discover the level of understanding by the operator. If the operator is unaware of a technical manual, maintenance guide, a checklist, or why a procedure or a tolerance range is important, it's usually a training issue.

**When one is detected, many are suspected.** If one operator is unaware of the technical aspects, it's a sure bet many in the organization are unaware of the approved process.

Often, information is passed along word of mouth versus using a reference for education and training. As a result, there is a practical drift from policy. Daily practice has drifted away from the approved policy and procedure - practical drift. I suspect you'll see the same thing with your plant's equipment maintenance unless you take pains to provide training and follow it up with inspections by managers schooled in inspecting. A short discussion about inspections follows.

## Leadership training in the Army identifies several reasons for inspecting:

*Determine if policies, procedures, and standards are being met.* The other reasons for inspecting are really complementary to this one. If the corporation has a new policy, how are you ensuring its implementation at all levels throughout the business? If you announce your goal is to reduce copy paper usage at corporate headquarters, how are you going to support, or enforce that measure? This is a story line in Chapter 7.

## Band of Brothers or Band of Inhibitors

Deming warns of the 'band of inhibitors.' These are the senior managers around the executive who filter information to him, and from him. One must understand this is going to happen and you must have a plan to defeat the situation.

Louis V. Gerstner, former CEO of IBM, and author of *"Who Says Elephants Can't Dance?"* discusses how he ensured information moved from his office to every employee and the method for gathering information from the rank-and-file members of IBM. **"All of this takes enormous commitment from the CEO to communicate, communicate, and communicate some more."**

*Determine if specific tasks are being completed on time to desired standards.* When you identify an action to be completed by a certain date or time with a quality standard described, make it a habit to follow up to ensure your team is complying with your directions. If you want to ensure the information flow from the executive suites is getting to the rank and file, talk to those lower-echelon employees about the subject. If they are unaware, move up the line until you determine who is filtering the information.

*Observe and study procedures and techniques.* Often it helps you understand the level of expertise, or potential shortcomings in your organization if you watch a process or a procedure yourself. Walking the Gemba. Take along the resident expert for a technical set of eyes. See if the safety features are used and policies are enforced. Watch the assembly of your products. Look for ways to improve. Look for deviations from the established policy. Where is quality control applied, throughout the process or only at the end?

Perhaps your employees have truly found a better way and the policy needs to change.

*Determine if items of equipment are present.* Sometimes you should inspect to ensure you have all the equipment you are supposed to have in an organization. Is every tool on hand? Is someone signed for the equipment? Is the paperwork up to date, or has the employee who signed for all the equipment left to take another job, or retired? Are the parts also included in sets, kits, and outfits?

A school system in a large city discovered they were missing a significant number of computers. There were records proving the computers were delivered from the supplier but that is where accountability stopped. When the auditors arrived, the computers couldn't be found. Losses through poor accountability can impact your businesses or taxpayers, dramatically.

*Determine probable combat effectiveness.* In the Army, readiness (for combat) is the name of the game, but corporations have parallel criteria. Are all your forklifts operational? Are there inoperable or missing parts that make a machine unsafe to operate? Are your delivery trucks up to date on services? Do you have a truck that didn't pass inspection and is now being used as an unofficial parts supply warehouse for the other vehicles?

*Assist in development of subordinate leaders.* In almost every action you undertake as a leader, you are developing the next generation of managers. If you cut corners, and take a casual attitude towards the corporate policies, safety, and maintenance this is the example that most subordinates will follow, regardless of your speeches to the contrary. In keeping the idea strictly focused on inspections, why is it important to the novice manager for the seasoned manager, or supervisor to inspect? The obvious reason is the seasoned manager should know considerably more about the product, the process, the equipment, or the policy than the novice.

## A Visit from Senior Management

Suppose you are preparing your plant for the visit of a senior executive. You've worked doubly hard and exercised extreme diligence in anticipation. You feel ready. The executive arrives, spends time with your employees on the line, makes a speech, and eats lunch with your management team.

In the out brief, he commends you on all the primary systems you manage, as you expected. You've got a good team. Then he identifies a few things you hadn't considered.

Unbeknownst to you, weeks ago, he and several team members called acting as interested customers getting a feel for the skills of those answering the phones, and ease a caller is connected with the right person. The inspection had already begun.

While driving into the industrial area where your operations are located, this executive looked for company signage, both directional and advertising. When he found signs, he looked at the age of the sign and freshness of the paint. Did the sign look worn or new? Was the sign upright or leaning precariously?

He looked for that stretch of highway that your plant is sponsoring for beautification. Does this stretch of highway reflect well on your organization, or did the initiative start as a great idea but lacks management interest now? Is your section of roadway covered in litter?

As he entered the parking area, he noticed the landscaping, flags and banners, presence of litter, and overall appearance of the facility. He surveyed the outside and inside as a realtor would. Did it have curb appeal? Would he be proud to work there?

During the plant visit, he looked for functioning light bulbs, painted safety stripes around the equipment, chains without chain guards, etc. When he had excused himself to wash his hands, he was inspecting the maintenance, stockage levels, and cleanliness of the restrooms. Throughout his visit, he was looking for hearing and eye protection in use by everyone.

He approached the inspection with the eyes, and skills, of a drill sergeant. He searched from top to bottom, left to right, front to rear, on the way in, and on the way out.

Restaurants teach an inspection technique known as the figure 8. You walk through the dining room; go through a door to the kitchen, walk around the kitchen, and return to the dining room. You are making a figure 8 as you survey the area. Afterwards, you visit the restrooms. Of course, before you walk inside, you inspect the outside…signage, lights, and litter.

After the seasoned manager's review of his observations, the novice manager develops a different perspective. The aperture regarding his responsibilities and corporate expectations has widened.

Are these outside, extraneous, details important factors for a business to manage? Consider your latest decision on a home improvement contractor, plumber, or electrician. Are you more apt to select someone who drives the van that looks disorganized, and has a faded paint job, or the company with the late model van with fresh signage?

General Jerry White explained that organizations have a veneer.

When you initially set up operations (a brigade in the field, or a new business in town) the unit or the owner, applies a thick veneer. Everyone looks at the site like a realtor might; examines it with fresh eyes. All the light bulbs work; the place is clean, organized, and litter free. The mirrors and windows have no smudges…no fingerprints. Everything is in its place.

After you move in, or begin operations, the area begins to look 'lived in'. A certain amount of sloppiness begins to creep in. The veneer begins to peel away. The inhabitants aren't as quick to replace a bulb or clean the mirrors. Overnight, it becomes an unattractive place. This is why leaders must look at their areas, every day with a new set of eyes. You need to have your mental (or written) checklist that requires your routine attention. See it with the eyes of a customer, potential partner, or a prospective employee.

A note about checklists: In WWII, seasoned pilots were being killed while testing the relatively complex 4-engine bombers. A checklist was developed. Enforcing the checklist reduced mishaps and fatalities. Checklists remain a part of an air crew's preflight operations.

A hotel patron noticed, when leaving one morning, a light had burned out in one of the nooks near the elevator. The light affected nothing; it wasn't lighting an area where there would be any foot traffic. Upon returning that evening, the hotel guest noticed the light bulb had been replaced. It was obvious that someone was looking to ensure all bulbs were operational.

As a jumpmaster, you are taught "not to look for what is wrong (with the parachute and equipment rigging); inspect to ensure everything is right." This mandate brings a slightly different perspective with it. When you are inspecting to ensure everything is correct, the incorrect will become glaringly apparent.

There is an old saying that soldiers **RE**spect the leader who **IN**spects what he **EX**pects. If you put out the word for an activity, standard, or expectation but you never check to see if anyone implemented the action, what did you really accomplish? After a few of your pronouncements with no efforts to follow up, don't be surprised when your organization no longer takes your mandates seriously and subsequently takes no action on them. If you expressed your **IN**tention, you must give the initiative your **AT**tention.

Or, as Gerstner says, **People don't do what you expect but what you inspect**.

Most employees really want to do a good job. When they aren't performing well, it's usually because of the training and awareness of the underlying reasons for an action. This is what we do, and this is why we do it…and do it this way. If they can do it correctly, but don't, that's another issue altogether.

A business consultant who worked in the textile industries in the Southeast reported one mill owner's in-depth understanding of mill operations. He was thoroughly engaged in production management, and machine efficiency. The owner expected good results and high output, but when he noticed there was an uncharacteristically high production rate for a significant time, at one of his mills, instead of growing excited, he became worried. He would deploy a no-notice team to check the maintenance of the equipment at that mill.

He realized equipment had to be taken offline to conduct maintenance. This should have been reflected in a lower production rate. When the rate remained high, and steady, it usually indicated someone was cutting corners on taking care of HIS equipment.

Performing maintenance on your equipment and applying thought to your maintenance program is a skill that is important in uniform, in a business suit, or when working on the factory floor. Neglecting maintenance can often lead to a catastrophic failure, and an industrial accident, often with injuries.

## A Lesson for Lieutenants

Unfortunately, not everyone becomes as well schooled, or disciplined in the maintenance program as those leaders who had worked for Bob Jackson. The knowledge acquired while studying at Jackson's Lyceum provided the background for a great object lesson to a group of future officers, one summer day.

A leader who had served under Jackson was selected for duty as an ROTC instructor. During the tour, he would spend every summer at ROTC Advanced Camp as a tactical officer (mentor and evaluator).

As a tactical officer, he was assigned to mentor a platoon of about 50 cadets from various universities. The platoon included a mix of those who wanted an active-duty Army career and those who also wanted to serve their nation, but intended to take the Reserve or National Guard route.

One morning, as several platoons organized themselves to load trucks that would take them to a rifle range; the Jackson-trained officer began talking with one of the young drivers supporting the ROTC cadet training. This soldier would be driving a truck designated to take part of the platoon to the range.

When asked how long the unit had been supporting ROTC camp. The young driver replied, "About six weeks." He was asked if he had performed PMCS that day. He responded, "Sir, that's not done in real units."

The Jackson alumnus continued to probe and asked how long had it been since the vehicle returned to the motor pool for regular maintenance. This line of inquiry revealed the truck had not been checked by the driver, nor serviced by mechanics since being dispatched, six weeks previously. ***When one is detected...*** In fact, none of the trucks had been serviced since being dispatched from the motor pool.

The tactical office directed his cadets to disembark and quickly introduced them to a few aspects of the Army's Maintenance Management System. He also informed the lieutenant colonel in charge of this cadet company of the maintenance situation and recommended hiking to the range instead of riding.

The colonel thought the tactical officer a bit rigid, perhaps harsh, but agreed that the Jackson-trained officer could march *his* platoon to the range. The rest of the company would ride. Surprisingly, the tactical officer reported the cadets weren't as excited by the prospect of marching to the range as he thought they should be. He also suspected there was a fair amount of conversation about his intellect and heritage as the cadets marched to the range.

As the platoon arrived at the rifle range, they were greeted by a most interesting scene. The bumper of one of the trucks was buried a few inches into the range shack. The brakes had failed on the truck, in which 20 cadets would have been riding. The truck could not make a full stop before it ran into the building. Fortunately, by the time it made contact with the building it had slowed considerably. Surprisingly, no one was hurt. The vehicle was hardly damaged. The wooden shack would need some repair. The situation became the perfect teaching point to 50 cadets who would be lieutenants or working in corporations in less than a year.

On the factory floor, assembly line, office, or be it in the motor pool or arms rooms, keeping the equipment running safely and extending its serviceable lifespan is an important value, and skill. Understanding how to operate the equipment, knowing the safety features, and the emergency procedures are all responsibilities managers should take seriously.

By learning all you can about your equipment you might avoid spending unnecessary funds for repairs when proper maintenance would have prevented the breakdown. By enforcing the maintenance, and safety, you avoid heartbreaking injuries to your team members when you have a *shuttle at your weaving mill fly out of the loom.*

Accidents come with a hefty price tag. The increased costs can come in several forms - federal disability premiums and health insurance premiums increase, while the good will of your uninjured teammates decreases. Worst of all, there is an injury to, or death of, a valued member of your team.

In the next chapter, you will be introduced to General Meloy and discover how he executed the transformation of a large, complex organization. His technique will also show you how to tie your systems together.

# Chapter 7

# Driving Transformation

Consider your good fortune if tapped to execute the turnaround of a poorly performing company. Or, conversely, your unfortunate predicament if moved into a senior executive position within your corporation and discover disturbing trends that had been covered up, or even perpetrated by your predecessor. Another situation played out too often finds you already the head of the local office; the employees are giving it their all; but the corporate headquarters informs you that if your numbers don't improve, the plant will be closed. Opportunities...and problems!

How do you undertake improving performance, or changing the culture or direction of a large, bureaucratic organization? How does one earn a reputation of change agent...a master of the turn around?

One could use the negative approach employed by a well-known change consultant for the Empire—Darth Vader. **"...Commander. I'm here to put you back on schedule."** (His techniques are not recommended.)

A review of Gerstner's *Who Says Elephants Can't Dance?* provides significant insights into senior executive actions during a turnaround.

Maybe you just want to adjust the level of excellence and upgrade performance in a great organization, or you've decided on a new corporate initiative. How would you ensure the success of your change strategy?

The larger the organization, the more difficult it is to make changes to accomplish a vision or undertake an initiative. In a very small company, the owner can make and implement a decision very quickly. The difference can be compared to a captain turning a large container ship around to that of a boatswain in an inflatable infiltration boat who must only command **left side back paddle; hold; give way together** to change direction.

In this chapter, you are going to look at driving change when you are the senior executive of a large organization. You will follow Major General Guy S. "Sandy" Meloy, III, who will serve as the primary practitioner, and exemplar.

If you are looking at the organization as if you're the sole proprietor and want it to reflect your character and your ideas of excellence, you should enjoy this chapter. You'll learn how to make that happen. You'll see how a great leader drives transformation.

Major General (MG) Meloy was well known for actions that earned him a Distinguished Service Cross in 1966, in OPERATION ATTLEBORO, in the Republic of South Viet Nam. Meloy, then a major, was commanding a battalion, a unit normally commanded by a lieutenant colonel, which is one rank higher.

His battalion was embroiled in a particularly rough fight and significantly outnumbered. More rifle companies were airlifted into the area. Eventually, he would command 11 rifle companies during the engagement. To add insight to this perspective, a battalion has only 3 rifle companies. Meloy was a major and was now maneuvering the forces that are doctrinally led by a brigade commander, a full (bird) colonel.

A few years…and promotions…later, Colonel Meloy commanded the 1st Brigade of the 82nd Airborne Division. This was the unit that habitually took the long view in preparing NCOs for increased responsibilities.

He was an innovative commander. With the United States still in the Cold War, Meloy analyzed the threat and developed plans for an airborne infantry unit fighting against large, armored forces in Europe.

Due to normal rotations and for his additional senior officer seasoning, Meloy left the brigade, only to return a few years later as the division commander, a Major General with two stars.

It took Meloy very little time to make his mark on the division. Obviously, his experience in running large organizations helped, and his recent experience commanding a brigade in the division acquainted him with the strengths and the weaknesses within the unit.

A note that may provide insight into his behavior as a senior executive:

After retirement, Meloy penned quite a few leadership articles for military journals. Apparent, throughout the articles, were his love of soldiers and sincere appreciation of the NCOs who mentored him when he was a young officer.

At the level where sergeants work, detail with regards to weapons and vehicles is extremely important. NCOs are also charged—perhaps not officially, but culturally—with training the lieutenants and captains who are assigned to the unit. Meloy had learned his lessons well and, more importantly, never forgot them. He never forgot the lessons, nor lost his respect for the NCOs. This respect revealed itself in meetings during his tenure as the commander of the 82nd.

Some may say when you are operating at the senior executive level, you shouldn't be concerned with details. You are allowing yourself to get too far down in the weeds. **"De minimis non curat praetor"** (the magistrate does not consider trifles). But consider this counter argument. In WWII, General Eisenhower was involved in the strategic planning of the cross-channel invasion, and liberation of Europe, but he took time to attend squad rehearsals.

Meloy realized there were topics not covered in the military schools at forts like Benning, Knox, Sill, and Huachuca. Certain technical information must be learned on the job and from those with whom or for whom you work. He was determined to ensure his officers received some burnishing while he was in charge.

As division commander, or CG (commanding general), he used his management wisdom, along with his vast technical expertise to fine tune the division. Like Jackson, Meloy significantly increased the level of competence in technical matters, among the officers and NCOs, as he showed them how the systems worked together.

As you read this, you might question whether this is truly a transformation. Granted, the division was already great. But the process he used to install changes, and create a directional change in culture is also how you could change a poorly performing organization. He began implementing change immediately, and within 6 months the culture had changed, and remained changed. The level of expertise in the interrelated systems had dramatically increased.

## Driving Change

Suppose you are sitting at your desk, or out on the assembly line one day, and the Jack Welch or Sandy Meloy of your corporation suddenly walks through the door, unannounced. He was touring plants and getting a feel for the organization and just stopped by to chat. He asks how things are going and you, being very motivated and conscientious, reply in positive, upbeat tones. He seems quite content. You can tell the boss loves being out of the headquarters and down where the product is made and shipped.

He casually invites you to tell him about your. . . *something obscure that goes on within the organization*, something that doesn't garner a whole lot of attention from you. As you uncomfortably reveal your ignorance on this topic, he asks a related question about a different topic, but asks it in a way that indicates these two subjects are somehow inextricably linked. After a second strike, he throws you a softball (easy question) that makes you feel you are going to survive this encounter.

When you respond with absolute certainty about Subject #3, he begins to show you how the question could only be answered correctly if you were intimately familiar with the answers he was looking for when he questioned you on subjects #1 and #2. Suddenly, you feel much more like Creon, in *Antigone,* than plant manager.

If a senior executive executed this ploy merely to show how smart he or she was, it would not be a tale worth repeating. Meloy used his questions to determine information, and to help you understand where you needed to increase your expertise for senior level leadership.

Instead of learning by sitting in a classroom, as instructors shovel the information in your direction, his technique allowed you to become actively engaged in the learning process. He also used this time to size you and your team up. Meloy would be assigning missions in combat and needed to know your strengths and weaknesses.

Much can be learned about someone's leadership potential by observing their responses to critical questioning. When asked a question does your subordinate equivocate, or provide direct truthful answers? One oft-neglected answer is, "I don't know, but I intend to find out immediately." And then, find out.

A lieutenant arrived for his first assignment just as the organization was preparing for a month-long deployment. The lieutenant was assigned to the mortar platoon. He had a great team of NCOs to keep him from going too far wrong.

During the first days in the field, his commander asked him how to perform misfire procedures when the mortar round was dropped down the tube and it didn't fire. The bomb was sitting…unexploded…at the bottom of the mortar tube. It is, obviously, a very serious situation, and the platoon leader has a key role in the process.

The lieutenant responded he didn't know. It was a proper response for a lieutenant, newly assigned to a mortar platoon. The commander suggested he find out.

The next day, the commander asked him the same question. The lieutenant reminded to the commander that he had already answered that question yesterday. The commander replied, "Yesterday, 'I don't know' was an appropriate answer, but 24 hours later, that answer is no longer acceptable."

He had been afforded 24 hours, and a team of excellent NCOs with whom he could have become competent in misfire procedures. Instead, he chose to waste the 24 hours. This was a key indicator of his potential, and initiative.

## A Visit from Meloy

Meloy would arrive, often unannounced, to your headquarters. After greetings, which included salutes and the unit motto, Meloy would get down to business and ask how everything was going in the battalion.

One day he visited the 508th Infantry. The greeting to senior officers in the 82nd Airborne Division is "All the Way, Sir!" It's an airborne greeting. It was even used in the movie *The Green Berets*, when John Wayne asks a platoon of paratrooper students running by, "How far?" Their response was, "All the way!"

In the 508th, the response to "All the Way" since its activation in WWII was "Red Devil." It seemed almost all questions could be satisfied with a strong, motivated - "Red Devil!" (By the way, in Jackson's battalion, the response was - "Rock Steady!" Rock Steady harkened back to a fight in September 1863, in which the 19th Infantry earned the moniker, Rock of Chickamauga in north Georgia.)

The 508th personnel would initially reply "Red Devil" to almost any question, it seemed. The commander gave the CG a rundown of activities. After a few minutes of conversation about the topics the 508th commander enjoyed discussing, Meloy would invite him to **"Tell me about your *mortar* training program."** (The interview described here concerns mortars. It could have been any weapon, piece of equipment, or tactical mission.)

Mortars were an oft-neglected weapons system. They are more like an artillery weapon (indirect fire) than infantry (direct fire) weapon. What was often the case is a senior leader wouldn't pay much attention to mortars, unless the leader had served in a mortar platoon as a young lieutenant. These senior officers quickly discovered this was unfortunate, because Sandy Meloy had been a mortar platoon leader in his much younger days.

As the battalion commander and operations officer would stammer for a response, with that deer-in-the-headlights look, Meloy would move on with his pick and shovel, prospecting for additional information.

"When did you last fire the mortars?" By this time the assistant S3, a sharp lieutenant standing in the background, would be digging through binders of lesson plans (those plans on which Jackson required such effort). (This was a time before computers became ubiquitous. Computers would have allowed him to conduct the fruitless search much faster…albeit with the same result.)

Although the young lieutenant was searching mightily through the records, he was, as was the commander and S3, all fairly certain that there would be no record of mortar training to find within the 3-ring binder records of Alpha, Bravo, Charlie, or the Combat Support Companies' training. To put this in perspective, that situation equates to about 14 mortars that had not been fired, in collective memory; 14 mortar squads that hadn't trained; and 4 mortar platoons that were being ignored.

Meloy continued. "Keep looking for the last time you fired live ammunition, lieutenant. What about gunner's exams? When did you last administer a gunner's examination?"

The lieutenant hadn't seen any entries indicating that activity either. In fact, neither he, the S3 nor Battalion Commander, were aware of a gunner's exam for mortars.

(A gunner's exam is a dry fire exercise in which each crewman on a mortar executes the adjustment of the tube (which determines the ultimate location of the explosion as the mortar round returns to earth) in a simulated combat environment. The grader (a more senior mortarman) executes the adjustments in reverse, to determine if the examinee has performed unerringly. Strict records are maintained…should be maintained).

By this stage, the primary response of *"Red Devil"* has totally vanished from the conversation.

Here comes the softball…the easy pitch.

## Mortar Readiness

Meloy asks the battalion commander about the mortar readiness (for combat).

Note: Every major weapons system, vehicle, aircraft, etc., status of training, and a few select low density skills are reported monthly from the rifle company to the Chairman of the Joint Chiefs of Staff (CJCS). The report informs the Chairman of the go-to-war readiness of major units like the 82nd. The whole process is taken quite seriously. Fudging the numbers on the Unit Status Report (USR) is a quick way to learn about the corporate world, or unemployment line, as your talents may no longer be needed in the uniformed services.

Fortunately, for this battalion, only two days before this visit, the battalion commander had gathered information about mortar readiness from his company commanders, consolidated it, and prepared the readiness report. The status was still fresh in his mind. This was a question he could answer with absolute certainty. He proudly informed the division commander his battalion mortars were 100% operationally ready.

At this point the commander was breathing a welcomed sigh of relief. The S3 had relaxed. The lieutenant had ceased his pointless search for nonexistent mortar training.

## A Systems Approach

As Meloy nodded his head, and smiled, he asked the commander if he realized that to report 100% on his mortars, a unit must fire live ammunition every quarter and conduct a monthly gunner's exam. Enter Creon, stage left.

As the thought of falsely reporting readiness sunk into all Red Devils nearby, Meloy continued his quest. Who are your mortar platoon leaders? (These lieutenants should be urging for training and keeping their company commanders informed of the requirements.)

The commander responded that because of shortages in officer assignments, the mortar platoon leader positions are going unfilled. Meloy follows up with, "You realize these are your most important platoons, don't you?" (Obviously, that was one of those subjects left off the syllabus at Fort Benning.) **"In combat, you request air support and you request artillery. You command mortars."** The artillery and Air Force can be working a higher priority mission. Your mortars must do what you require.

Jackson used this same comment often. He felt the same way. For both, the importance of mortars was something they had learned in the jungles of Viet Nam. Another Jackson alumnus who served in Afghanistan, and rose to 3 stars before retiring, had remembered Jackson's words and heeded his advice.

Meloy's demeanor changes a bit - more collegial - and he asks the battalion commander to summon his company commanders, the 1SGs, the mortar platoon sergeants, and the S1 (personnel officer). As they all moved into the conference room, one could tell Meloy was absolutely comfortable with the NCOs. (Some leaders in organizations aren't particularly comfortable in a social situation with the line personnel, although the great ones generally are.)

Meloy asked the assembled crowd about the gunner's exams. Surprising the officers who were present, the NCOs produced the score cards. Although the NCOs had been unsuccessful in getting the requirement on the training schedule, they had been fencing time and conducting the exams. They recognized its importance. Their activity and this work-around didn't look good for the officers, but Meloy must have suspected it was happening. Perhaps a meeting like this is how he learned about it from his NCOs, long ago.

Meloy suggested the unit leaders compare the crew scorecards with the unit manning report (UMR). In early days of computer usage, the UMR was a tissue-thin, difficult-to-read roster prepared on dot matrix printers. It listed each job in a unit, and who was filling the position.

The S1, maybe to take some heat off the commander, reported to the CG that the division headquarters prepared and published this document and that the battalion wasn't really to blame for it not accurately reflecting the assignments within the battalion. It was a valiant effort by the subject matter expert in personnel administration. Unfortunately, he was absolutely wrong; or as Churchill might say, **"Loosely educated."**

The division commander schooled the assembled leaders on how the process is designed to work. A new trooper (replacement) arrives in the division and is assigned to a battalion. The name is entered on the UMR for that battalion, but the position is just a placeholder. The commanders, 1SGs, and S1s are responsible for assigning the new trooper to a specific job. It is also their responsibility to submit the changes to the division headquarters. They were also responsible for the electronic adjustments to keep the UMR up-to-date with subsequent changes such as promotions and job changes within the battalion.

With the monthly run of the key punch cards, the positions on the UMR reflected the truth as the computer (or clerk at division headquarters) knew it. But the reality of crew assignments should also be reflected in the examination score cards. His point: training is tied to the personnel system, in addition to the readiness system.

Meloy asked the mortar sergeants for their bore-sighting information and aiming circle calibrations. (The aiming circle is a sophisticated compass used to lay (position and align) the mortars when occupying a firing position. Remember the model unit training example in Chapter 5?) The platoon sergeants had the records readily available. The maintenance cards for mortars reflected the number of rounds each tube had fired in its lifecycle.

Meloy asked the commanders if they knew how bore-sighting and calibration are reflected in the USR. They did not. Meloy tied still another system into the one weapon he had begun investigating.

Returning to the topic of officer assignments, Meloy asks, "If you aren't staffing your mortar platoon with officers, can I assume you aren't conducting Mortar Safety Officer Courses, either? Would that be right?" It was a correct assumption. The officers were unaware of the requirement. Meloy was tying still another system—safety—into an investigation of just one weapon in their arsenal.

Meloy's excavation wasn't complete until he discussed the inventory of the mortars, and the smaller parts that sometimes are neglected during changeover inventories. One more system—supply and accountability—and its impact on the single weapon that began the conversation, was revealed to those present.

Before leaving to energize another battalion, Meloy instructed the unit to get smart on their weapons and the USR requirements. He suggested they dig into the reporting criteria to understand fully what is supposed to be evaluated and reported. He expected them to get better with mortars, and he would be back.

Before he departed from the visit, Meloy spent a few minutes assuring the 508th leadership team he already knew most of the answers before he arrived. Their situation was all too common throughout the division and he intended to change things. Although chastised, they were encouraged to make the necessary changes to come up to his standards.

Immediately, the 508th commander reported this instructive (painful) meeting to the Brigade Commander and to friends up and down Ardennes (the road on which the battalions of the 82nd Airborne Division are headquartered). They began serious investigations into the USR, UMR, and mortar requirements and, with those results, established an effective mortar training program.

Throughout his tenure as commanding general, Meloy invested the greater part of each day visiting the battalions, investigating and educating. The division became experts in mortar training.

A few weeks later, Meloy returned to Red Devil headquarters. This time, the battalion was ready. The UMR accurately reflected the assignments for every Trooper and officer in the battalion. They had dissected each entry in the USR and knew the criteria for 100% readiness, exactly, and what would cause the readiness rating to drop. The training records, organized by crew, and UMR were accurate and up-to-date. They had conducted a safety officer course. Each safety officer had participated in at least one live fire. Every platoon was led by an officer, who was also certified as a mortar safety officer. Mortar training activities were indicated by index tabs in the training schedule binders.

As Meloy sprung from his jeep and approached, the battalion commander, looking confident, snapped a salute as he said, "All the Way, Sir!" Meloy looked around, knowing he was now seeing a better, more knowledgeable, confident group of soldiers, turned to the battalion commander and said with his schoolboy, mischievous grin, "Tell me about your machine gun training." This time around, the meeting was much more relaxed, and entertaining. The change he wrought in professionally administering, and managing the battalion was dramatic.

Major General Meloy quickly increased the level of competence in his officers by tutoring them in the technical aspects of their management jobs. He was also ever present in the field, just as Major General Kroesen and the others had been. As Meloy built fires (in a good way) under everyone for mortars and machine guns, he was performing the same magic in artillery and vehicles. By showing, with one weapon, how all the systems relate and how to fix the errors, the leadership teams were repairing the problems for all the systems (weapons, radios, vehicles, etc.)

You can empathize with the leaders of this organization. After you are 'caught short' in not understanding one line of a readiness report, you research every line. When you fix the mortar crews on the UMR; you also adjust the machine gun and anti-tank crews; radio telephone operators (RTOs); etc. Meloy's assistant division commanders (brigadier generals) were doing the same with their portfolios—support and training.

The lesson on change management is that you can accomplish significant changes to the organization's values and activities by asking questions and digging into the answers; understanding how all the systems are interrelated; creating discomfort in those who aren't executing to standard; or have neglected to adopt the new initiatives. Asking questions helps you identify who should be on the bus and those who need to exit at the next stop.

## Jackson on Mortars

Jackson personally authored a document to explain his training program. This is part of the paragraph on mortars: "**Mortars are the only indirect fire assets we command. They are the most responsive indirect asset and must be used routinely. Mortar crews must be 100% filled with qualified personnel and backup personnel must be trained. Leaders must ensure that squads and platoons perform to standard. Routinely, the Battalion will administer a Mortar Safety Officer / NCO Course to certify Indirect Fire Safety Officer and NCOs.**" You can appreciate that had he been questioned by Meloy, the information exchange would have been decidedly different.

Administrative discipline is often reflected, or impacts, tactical and training discipline.

As General George S. Patton would say, "**There is only one sort of discipline - PERFECT DISCIPLINE. Men cannot have good battle discipline and poor administrative discipline.**"

How Can You Apply the Questioning Technique to Drive Change?

Imagine you've discovered that sexual harassment, or some other ethical problem has been allowed to exist in the corporation you've been hired to lead. You explain in the executive suite, in no uncertain terms, that "we must fix this." When meeting with your direct reports and ask about their goals and objectives, you instruct them to put their efforts to end sexual harassment among the top three items in which you intend to assess them and recommend bonuses.

You can't stop there. Whenever you visit a plant, you inquire. "Tell me about the Sexual Harassment program. Show me what you are doing. What have you heard about my feelings on this matter?" (Find out if the word is getting below your band of inhibitors.) Ask the supervisors and employees on the factory floor and on the loading dock how they feel, and what they know about the Sexual Harassment program. "When did you hear about it? What are the action steps? What are their reporting responsibilities?"

When it comes to communicating new visions or directions, I've heard it compared to driving a large nail through a 6X6 beam.

It would take an awfully strong person, with a heavy hammer, a steady eye, hitting the nail just right for it to go through the beam with just one hit. However, if you give a six-year-old the hammer, nail, and 6X6, and allow the child enough whacks and enough time, the nail can be hammered through the beam.

To present your idea in such an effectual manner to enjoy a Pentecostal moment, you must hit the nail just right, with the right force. For most communication, the only way to succeed in creating the desired change is to continually, routinely pound on the nail until we drive the message home. (...while employing the action items required.) Communicators must be more like Paul, the Apostle, than Peter, the Disciple.

## An Easier Problem to Study

Consider this more finite problem, or opportunity, and see how it might be addressed using various methods. Suppose you are the senior manager in a division within your corporation. One weekend, your teenage daughter, the staunch environmentalist, challenges you to use less paper at your office. She convinces you of the merits of her idea by tossing into the argument a word about the cost savings this will provide.

In your Monday morning assembly with all employees, you announce you are undertaking...nay...*the division* is undertaking a new cost-saving, environmentally-friendly position in the use of copy paper. The division is committed to saving money, and trees, from this day forward. You notice while some heads are nodding, in some heads eyes are rolling. Some attendees are taking notes and others are not.

Fast forward, three months later. Since the initial announcement, you've not said another word about this paper saving crusade. That weekend, your daughter, home for a visit from college, asks about your progress. You sheepishly admit, you'll have to get back to her on that subject. You feel you've let her down.

At the next Monday morning staff meeting, attended by your direct reports, you ask about the progress on paper savings. What do you suppose the answers will be? There will probably be scant progress, if anyone even remembered the announcement at the Monday morning assembly that happened three months ago.

## A Different Approach

Rewind to the week after the original assembly. At the staff meeting with your direct reports, you remind them of last week's announcement and the division's commitment. You inquire, "Who has developed their plan for reducing paper usage?" (Now they understand you really expect some action.) This will probably be the first time they have thought about your comments since the day of the announcement.

## Another Approach (Logical and Emotional)

Rewind to the week <u>after</u> the first assembly, again. In the morning assembly (before the staff meeting), you remind every employee of your commitment; you show the figures for paper usage for last year and this year, to date. You show the same information but its equivalence in trees, with an average size of 'x diameter by y height'. You describe the problem in its equivalence in acreage of normal timber forests, and the years it takes to replace the wood used to produce the amount of paper the organization used last year. You show a table of copy paper usage by sections, within this division. You ask for volunteers to brainstorm ideas for reducing paper usage.

In your follow-on staff meeting with your direct reports, you show the tables again, and ask them to start working on plans to reduce the paper usage. Midweek, you host the brainstorming session using an outside facilitator. You excuse yourself from the meeting to encourage a free flow of information. At the end of the week as you roam around the offices, you ask each of your chiefs to talk to you about their plans.

During the week you notify your chiefs to be prepared to discuss paper and ink usage: last year; this time last year; last quarter; and this time last quarter; along with their initiatives. These tables will become a part of the routine staff meeting, effective immediately. And you direct them to add paper cost reduction as one of their objectives on this year's performance goals.

At the next staff meeting, you invite the facilitator and the leader of the brainstorming team to report the recommendations agreed on by them. You ask the team leader for those ideas that were suggested but considered too outlandish by the brainstorming team. You want to review them. Often, rank-and-file employees might consider an idea too costly, or not acceptable, while the senior executive might not.

At the next Monday assembly, you publicly commend the team for the ideas, and on that day, you begin to implement recommendations from the brainstorming session.

One recommendation, regarding the substitution of the server for paper, requires everyone to develop the habit (discipline) to save things on the network server instead of in personal sites. To ensure this is done, you require every section and program to apply the file name and file path to digital documents. This way you (your information technology [IT] section) can ensure the habits are being formed. You arrange for electronic notebook briefings and enforce the reduction in your own office, and on your own machines.

In this age of the computers and the capability of perfecting briefings and other reports, there's a tendency to continually change words and commas right up until the last minute. And then change it again, after the briefing based on the senior executives wishes. A large volume of paper and ink cartridges can be consumed if discipline, rigor, and expectations are not imposed.

The personnel of one organization would prepare a binder full of color briefings for routine daily meetings and specialty meetings. On average, there were 10 attendees at each meeting requiring at least 12 binders, one for each attendee, one for the briefer, and one for record keeping. Very few attendees wanted to keep the paper copies. Following each meeting the presentations were discarded (shredded).

The organization calculated the cost of paper, ink, binders, and dividers and invested in electronic notebooks. As each briefing was finalized, the electronic notebooks would be loaded for the attendees. Using electronic notebooks instead of paper copies saved money and significant time that had been used (wasted?) in preparing binders and shredding documents.

### Returning to your paper saving crusade

Of the three approaches:

- An announcement with no follow up,

- An announcement with some follow up, and

- An announcement, followed by a second, including logical information (costs of paper and ink) and emotional hooks. Emotional hooks might include visual information (numbers of trees, acres of forests, years of growth). Plus engagement with the brainstorming team and implementing ideas from their list and keeping the information in front of the organization routinely, tracking improvement.

Which approach is most likely to succeed? You know, without a doubt.

Admiral Hyman G. Rickover, the Father of the Nuclear Navy, said, "**A good manager must have unshakeable determination and tenacity. Deciding what needs to be done is easy; getting it done is more difficult. Good ideas are not adopted automatically. They must be driven into practice with courageous impatience. Once implemented, they can be easily overturned or subverted through apathy or lack of follow up, so a continuous effort is required. Too often, important problems are recognized but no one is willing to sustain the effort needed to solve them.**"

Embrace his phrase *courageous impatience.*

### Production Plant Improvements

In Eliyu Goldratt's *The Goal*, the plant manager has returned to his hometown to run the company plant, a major employer in a small town. As the story unfolds, he is informed the corporate office intends to shutter the plant if there is no significant improvement. Goldratt takes you through the change process, in a novel way. In the story, you learn about the theory of constraints and how to unblock the log jams. If you are faced with this situation, dig into this book, and see if the situation and the solution apply.

## Another word about Major General Meloy

In updating the practices of the 82nd Airborne Division, he tasked the units to provide subject matter experts (SMEs) representing all ranks and skills, to develop new standing operating procedures (SOPs) for two of its primary operations—deploying the division and conducting parachute operations. The two were connected and these documents provided guidance on the distinct elements of each. Using personnel with actual, and recent experience, he charged the division staff with preparing up-to-date, effective 'how-to' manuals.

By tapping the brainpower of personnel throughout the division, instead of relying on his core (and generally overworked) staff at division headquarters, he implemented the inclusive brainstorming technique Colonel Katz employed. Even those who weren't selected to help influence these documents knew at least one of their buddies who had been selected. This technique resulted in an immediate buy-in by most personnel.

Of course, Meloy wasn't one to stop at publishing a recipe for action. He, and his assistant division commanders, became conversant in each SOP. They would routinely visit a step in the process to discuss the SOP (quiz the leadership team on site), to ensure everyone was aware and following the new procedures, (again, walking the Gemba).

The Advanced Airborne School (AAS), where jumpmasters and load planners were trained, was required to immediately adopt and teach the updated procedures. A special assembly, of all experienced jumpmasters and load planners in the division, was convened at which Meloy introduced the new documents. The AAS instructors schooled everyone on the updated procedures.

The new procedures were routinely evaluated by members of the division staff to ensure jumpmasters and other leaders understood, and complied with, the updated procedures. Smart brigade commanders were implementing parallel training and evaluations. Meloy continued to have the events evaluated until the reports became universally favorable regarding understanding and complying with the updated procedures. Develop the standard and standardize the process throughout the enterprise.

As a jumpmaster, it was important to be at least as knowledgeable as the Commanding General on your responsibilities, especially when he arrived unannounced to jump from your aircraft. The new procedures had become part of the unit's DNA.

Meloy drove change through inclusive brainstorming; judicious questioning; preparing for and conducting routine visits; and engaging in follow up by him, his leadership team, and his staff.

### How can you, a senior executive, probe areas in which you aren't expert?

Suppose you aren't an expert in assembly line activities. You rose to prominence through marketing and sales. How do you become expert enough to question a plant manager? Have a conversation with an expert. Have your team put together a traveling book (electronic or binder). Discover how you should inspect. What are some questions to ask? What are the answers you should be hearing? Prepare before you visit. Have the expert accompany you for the second set of eyes. Have a plan for improving the situation, even if you aren't the expert.

### The Questioning Technique

In consultative selling, questions begin at a high level, and begin moving from general to more specific, and quite often end with yes-no (binary) questions. One technique to remember is the TED process. **T**ell me about…**E**xplain…and **D**escribe.

For example: Meloy started with…Tell me about. This is very open ended and the commander could have gone in any direction with the discussion. After this topic was exhausted by the commander, Meloy asked more specifically…When did you…? How are you…?

Asking questions to uncover information is a valuable skill as a leader. Learn how to uncover issues.

Deming on questions: **"If you don't know how to ask the right questions, you discover nothing."**

Examining the words **UN**cover, and **DIS**cover one might assume that true information must begin in a natural state of being *covered* and only by asking the questions do we reveal, *uncover*, or *discover*.

In the next chapter, there are tips for delegating. We'll approach delegation from the position you are responsible for everything your organization does or fails to do. To get more done, finish more projects, or call people for more appointments, you must work harder, smarter, and longer, or learn to delegate better. (You may still have to work harder, smarter, and longer but you'll increase productivity exponentially instead of arithmetically by learning to delegate and follow up skillfully.)

There is a belief by good leaders about delegation. Managing is much like parenting. You can delegate but you can't abdicate, nor can you abrogate your responsibilities.

## One last word about paper usage and forests...

Consider the impact (buy-in by your employees) if you quantified paper usage in trees and computed the number of trees required to frame a 1000 square foot home. How many homes could be framed by redirecting the use of wood from paper in your part of the corporation to 2X4s? Challenge the offices to reduce paper use. If it meets with your corporate values and policy perhaps you agree to convert a percentage of the savings to supporting construction of homes for the less fortunate.

# Chapter 8

# Delegation

One of the more difficult skills and disciplines to develop, but absolutely necessary for executive level success, is the art and science of delegating. It seems doubly difficult when you are an acknowledged expert (truly a wizard) in the field in which you must delegate. If you find yourself working late every night after others have left, and you're working through the weekends, you might want to develop your knowledge, skills, and abilities in, and the habit of, delegating.

### Fight the Do It Yourself (DITY) Urge

You worked hard to become a specialist, a subject matter expert (SME) in an area of high interest to the corporation. Your talents were recognized, and you were moved from bench chemist to a member of management. Early in your tenure in management an issue comes to your attention that is right up your alley. It becomes tempting to do the work yourself. It takes personal discipline to delegate the task to someone who is probably less competent and definitely less experienced at this juncture in his or her career. You tell yourself, "I can knock this requirement out quickly, and I know it will be correct." It's a siren song, but to develop your staff, and expand your span of control, you must be willing to delegate.

Invest more time in thinking about the work, discussing it with your team, and allow them to take part in the effort. Remember, one of your most important responsibilities is to develop your team members.

Another area in which you might need to fight the urge to do the work yourself, are those situations when a topic is presented that really piques your interest. You genuinely want to learn more about the subject. As a manager, one must conscientiously weigh the work and its impact on the organization. Where is the best application of your efforts?

As Rod Serling of *The Twilight Zone* might say, "**For your consideration…**" There is probably a good reason Jack Welch is not universally recognized as a leader in the chemical engineering field. I suspect it is because he learned to manage projects and his time, possibly overcoming a strong desire to work on individual problems that presented themselves, after he moved into management.

In Atlanta, Georgia, there is a chemical company in which the CEO actually started out as a bench chemist. Several times throughout his rise to CEO, he worked to reinvent himself.

From chemist, he was moved to sales and marketing. To support the transition, he attended courses focused on the knowledge, skills, and abilities required for success in calling on, and satisfying customer needs.

Ultimately, he was selected as CEO, and again there were skills and subjects about which he was unfamiliar. He reinvented himself again through study, discipline, and personal development.

One must adopt and learn new skills throughout your work life. A warning one should occasionally read is, "**What got you there, won't keep you there.**"

## Delegate or Assign

Delegation does not equate to merely assigning tasks. The manager, who delegates, remains 100% responsible for the quality and timeliness of the delegated task. The one executing the task is the manager's 'delegate' to the action.

On the other hand, a professor, who assigns a term paper, is not responsible for the quality of the work, or meeting the suspense. The student is. Assigning a task, even if you are very specific with expected results is not, exactly, the same as delegating.

When a manager delegates a task, there can be a wide range of supervision of, and autonomy allowed, along the management sliding scale. This oversight autonomy balance is based on experience and previous performance of the employee to whom the task is delegated, weighted against the complexity of the task. Regardless of who is selected, and how it was assigned, the manager remains responsible.

Management and fighting the urge to personally complete the work can be compared to parenting. Delegating well also has parallels in teaching in the early classroom years.

## Avoid doing the work of your children.

One of our major goals as a parent should be to ensure the child is ready to leave the nest and succeed in the adult world. Parents are also eager to ensure the child does extremely well in every aspect of growing up, and not suffer any measure of embarrassment in their journey to adulthood. These two goals can often be in competition. In addition, parents might feel they are being graded by their peers on the child's performance.

When finding your child struggling late at night over a last-minute science project, or a woodcarving project for Scouts, there can be a temptation to jump in and provide *just a little bit of assistance.*

This situation can quickly evolve (devolve?) into one in which the parent has moved to the garage, standing at a band saw, laboring at the project, and meticulously cutting out an awesome race car, while the child has moved over to the television or is playing games on his or her mobile device.

While not advocating free range children as a parenting method, parents might consider allowing a bit of embarrassment to spur the creative juices, and spark that innate industry gene necessary for success for later projects, and life. They'll get over the embarrassment. Like the leaders visited by MG Meloy, no one likes to feel the embarrassment of being caught short but it can be an effective goad to better performance.

Surely, it's important to assist in your child's development but it's less important to ensure they get an "A" on every assignment or win the wooden auto race. It might be more helpful, in the long run, to ensure your children develop an early, unambiguous understanding that Senior Management in your house is not going to bail them out of a homework jam or take on their responsibilities for the science project.

Of course, we also don't want a situation to develop into learned helplessness like the elephant who feels it is impossible to pull from the ground the stake to which he is tied. You don't want to set up a situation in which your subordinates or your children feel they cannot succeed.

## A Monkey on Your Back

To translate that to the workforce: When an employee has a problem preventing him from completing his work, after listening attentively to their tale, you might consider responding in this way... *"What are you planning to do about it? Talk to me about your plan. Have you brainstormed it with your team?"*

One colleague took a problem to the boss whose response was, **"Do you want my sympathy, or advice?"** Ouch.

Even if you have encountered hundreds of similar situations as the one being presented by one of your subordinates, and you have developed a few sure-fire approaches to solve the problem, fight the urge to provide a solution. I'm not suggesting this is a means of developing your reputation of being the tough boss. Instead, always be thinking about your employee's development. How can you best engage your employees in thinking through the issue and coming up with their own, possibly better, ideas? Work with your employees on their skills in problem solving, not on solving their problems.

You've put the question to the employee - *What are you planning to do about it?* After allowing the employee to exhaust their list of possible solutions, now it might be appropriate to suggest a few thoughts about techniques that have worked for you in the past. Remember Steve Adkins's counsel to the new insurance agent.

Like the baby sea turtle returning to the ocean, or the butterfly squeezing out of the cocoon, the struggle is important for growth.

## What if the process becomes normal behavior?

Another lesson Jackson tried to instill in his leadership team: Consider what your life will be like and how the organization will operate, if your approach and solution becomes the standard. Consider this with any problems that surface. Imagine that from this day forward, all employees will act in the same manner and all similar problems will be handled in the same way. Will that be a good thing?

If you are too quick to jump in and assist, you'll find yourself standing at the bandsaw (figuratively) every night. Meanwhile, your employees are heading to the parking lot at the end of the day. At the first hiccup, they come to you for a solution, and you accept the monkeys that were on their backs. You end up with an in-box full of monkeys and you grow angry at the work force as you see them file out of the door and into the parking lot to go home.

Your solution to the situation (not the solution to the problem presented to you) must be good for the short term and for the long term. It should send the signal to the others how problems will be solved.

## Professor or Teacher

Contrast the college professor, from a few paragraphs above, who assigns the term paper, with the middle school teacher who is teaching the students how to *organize* their work to complete a term paper. The middle school teacher's method is much more akin to delegating. (With apologies to all teachers if these elements are completely out of sequence, or a dozen more have been omitted.)

The teacher explains to the class what is expected in a term paper or book report. She, or he, identifies a date, maybe a week later, on which each student must have selected a topic, or book. Much like the Motor Pool Sergeant of an earlier chapter, the teacher has begun to put the students on her schedule (or his).

Showing the calendar, the teacher continues, pointing to the date the outline must be completed, and submitted. Next, the teacher identifies the date on which the first draft is to be submitted, and the expectations for that step in the process.

Possibly, the teacher explains what will happen with the first drafts (the teacher's review) before the papers are returned for additional editing or content development. Finally, the teacher points to the calendar on which the date is circled in red and announces the final due date. By structuring the work and setting clear dates for the completion along the process, the teacher has helped defeat the 'term paper mentality' discussed by Goldratt in *Critical Chain*.

The teacher has described the tasks; illustrated what success looks like; emplaced suspense dates all along the way to delivery date; and described expectations of a midpoint review. These activities are much like those of the manager who delegates the task.

## Closing the Base; Delegating the Tasks

So, if the skill—the art and science—of delegating is so important, how does one become effective in delegation management?

Return to the base closure project or imagine you have been tasked with closing a factory and moving to another state. Determine if the activities initiated by one of the senior members of the management team is worth emulating.

## Review the Plan of Action and Milestones

From the POA&M, the manager extracts all the tasks that are his responsibilities and are due within the next 6 weeks. He finds 10 tasks assigned to him.

The manager reviews the tasks and decides he must complete one of those tasks, personally. Nine of the tasks can be delegated. (Bear in mind the tasks can be delegated, but not the responsibility.)

Each task has a different degree of complexity. Several have early due dates; others won't be due until the end of the 6 weeks. The manager is familiar with the workload of personnel in the shop; is aware of the strengths and weaknesses of his team members; and considers the impact on ongoing projects, and family dynamics. (One might not want to assign a task to someone that takes them out of the town when that family is preparing for an imminent addition.) The manager reviews the tasks due beyond the initial six weeks to see when other tasks will become due.

Investing time on the front end, the manager thinks about each task and how success should be described, at the finish line. What will success look like?

Have you attended a meeting at which the manager seems to be thinking through (for the first time) the project as he stands in front of the team? Some managers seem to need an audience, to think. Discipline yourself to do your thinking (not all of it, of course) in advance. One general officer who had a real handle on running large complex organizations, would often remark **"Sometimes you have to slow down, to speed up."** Take time to study the problem and develop the solution, then execute quickly.

Assemble the team and discuss the plan. Gather input. Assign the tasks, schedule one-on-one reviews with each member of the team who has been assigned a task.

## Insurance Policy and Premiums

When you delegate a task, you must take out an insurance policy. **You must pay the premiums and keep them up to date.** What are the premiums? These are the conversations you have with the one to whom you delegated, and your out-of-the-office visits to see for yourself, the progress being made. You must be committed to following up and attending the meetings. Those are the premiums to ensure the tasks are completed to your standards.

At the personal interview, you discuss the mission, your vision and intent regarding the task you are delegating. You encourage the give and take discussion about all aspects of the task; identify the suspense dates, and your expectations.

Adjusting the level of oversight, based on the relationship with the employees and proven performance, you will probably ask that they return with a plan within a few days. You want to ensure they are on the right track from the beginning. The quality of the work is often a reflection of the quality of the guidance.

Set expectations for their response to a roadblock, and when to bring it to your attention. Ensure they keep an up-to-date folder on the server or their desk, so someone else can assume the task if the employee takes another job, requires emergency surgery, or is transferred from your office.

After the initial personal interview and task discussion, schedule a consolidated review convened at the same time (weekly, every other week, monthly) on the same day of the week with those to whom you have delegated tasks. Establishing a rhythm helps everyone with their calendar organization. Some of those who have been assigned tasks may be at different locations. It seems easier on the support staff to book teleconferences if the meetings have a routine—every Friday, at 2 p.m.

Much like Jackson's milestone meetings, this assembly is for your benefit. Remember, ultimately, you are responsible for the quality of the work and meeting the suspense dates and you want to model meeting discipline to your team.

## Micromanaging

Where does good follow up end and micromanagement begin? You won't find a textbook solution here. Healthy follow up may be described in this way: The manager shows up routinely. It's not a bizarre, out-of-the-ordinary situation when she walks into the office, or on the shop floor. She asks about your progress on the task. She dives into the issue, sometimes deeply, but doesn't take on the work. She doesn't drop down under your level to give instructions to one of your people in support of the assignment. You never feel blindsided by her activities with your team. She deals directly with you on issues, although she is comfortable talking with your personnel about the project. In her conversations with the workforce, her focus is on magnifying the importance of the task, and their contribution to the solution.

She holds you (the manager) 100% responsible but respects your position as the 'sole proprietor' of your shop. She doesn't undermine your authority and position. She never takes over the helm. Unless there is an issue of safety, in which sight, life, or limb is at risk, she never inserts herself between you and your team.

Micromanagement, conversely, violates these norms.

In *The Goal*, as the story begins, Goldratt relates an event where a senior manager visits the production plant and begins giving directions to the plant manager's subordinates, without talking with the plant manager. The chaos that results is instructive.

Jackson 'wrote paper' (performance evaluations) on few personnel in the organization—the five company commanders, deputy battalion commander (called the executive officer, or XO); and the senior enlisted advisor, the command sergeant major (CSM). Jackson's reputation, and the respect he generated, was in large measure a reflection of his effectiveness in working through, and developing, his subordinate managers.

When Jackson had an assignment for the staff, he discussed it with the XO. If he observed an egregious violation by a member of one rifle company such as a Charlie Company soldier walking around with his hands in his pockets, walking past litter on the ground, or not wearing a hat while outside, Jackson discussed that 'slippery slope to anarchy' with the Charlie Company commander. When an NCO issue confronted him, he talked with the CSM. All other conversations Jackson held with the 600 employees, throughout the two years he commanded, were convivial. He didn't give instructions to the 593 others who didn't work directly for him. He worked through a system the military calls the chain of command.

## Jethro, the Patron Saint of Business Consultants

Maybe the first recorded incident of an out-of-town business consultant advising a leader was Jethro, the father-in-law of Moses, in Exodus 18. He arrived to find Moses sitting in judgment in matters the people brought to him. (From the New American Bible)

The next day Moses sat in judgment for the people, while they stood around him from morning until evening.

When Moses' father-in-law saw all he was doing for the people, he asked, "What is this business you are conducting for the people? Why do you sit alone while all the people have to stand about you from morning till evening?"

Moses answered his father-in-law, "The people come to me to consult God. Whenever they have a disagreement, they come to me to have me settle the matter between them and make known to them God's statutes and instructions."

"What you are doing is not wise," Moses' father-in-law replied. "You will surely wear yourself out, both you and these people with you. The task is too heavy for you; you cannot do it alone. Now, listen to me, and I will give you some advice, and may God be with you. Act as the people's representative before God, and bring their disputes to God.

Enlighten them in regard to the statutes and instructions, showing them how they are to conduct themselves and what they are to do.

But you should also look among all the people for able and God-fearing men, trustworthy men who hate dishonest gain, and set them over the people as commanders of thousands, of hundreds, of fifties, and of ten. Let these render decisions for the people in all routine cases. Every important case they should refer to you, but every lesser case they can settle themselves.

Lighten your burden by letting them bear it with you! If you do this, and God so commands you, you will be able to stand the strain, and all these people, too, will go home content."

Moses listened to his father-in-law and did all he had said. He picked out able men from all Israel and put them in charge of the people as commanders of thousands, of hundreds, of fifties, and of tens. They rendered decisions for the people in all routine cases. The more difficult cases they referred to Moses, but all the lesser cases they settled themselves.

Then Moses said farewell to his father-in-law, who went off to his own country.

If you make all the corrections yourself, you'll find yourself overworked. Your team will grow frustrated as they wait, as you work through your in-box to render decisions.

If you choose not to delegate, then you will be doing the work, and staying late every night while the others are clearing the threshold at 5 p.m. Here is idea for you to think about: People are more invested and committed in an organization when they are given meaningful work. The more you can spread the important work among your direct reports, the higher morale generally climbs.

## Summary:

Honing your delegation skills:

- Select the tasks to delegate, and to whom you are going to delegate.

- Meet with the employee to discuss the task, their commitments, your commitments, and your vision and intent. (Think before you meet.)

- Commit to keeping your premiums up to date (in-office meetings, and visits where the action takes place).

- Remember, you are responsible for the quality and timeliness of the task.

One of the most enlightening projects the leadership team completed under Jackson was the 24- month plan. Discussed several times throughout this book, it reflected so many areas of his management behavior. The next chapter is devoted to the preparation of the 24-month plan. We'll discuss the process and the product, and how the plan was used, and updated, throughout the next two years of Jackson's command, in managing the major muscle movements of the organization.

Observations on effective personal and group level communication will be included in Chapter 10. If you make it a habit to talk regularly one-on-one with those for whom you are responsible, they tend to be more responsive when you need them to deliver on short notice. This is especially important with those who work at locations other than at the home office.

Communications (relationships) are like bank accounts. Every communication to provide information and engage in conversation about them, is a deposit. Every time you call to ask for a report, or do some work that is needed by you, their higher headquarters, but not necessarily of apparent value at their level, is a withdrawal. As long as you are making lots of deposits (sincere deposits) you won't be bouncing checks with your team.

In Chapter 11, you will revisit the base closure project. The various threads will be tied together that were unraveled throughout the book as you explored executive level project management.

The last chapter is titled Stray Voltage—a few tips and ideas to help you plan, organize, lead, and control...or manage at the executive level. Included will be good stuff that does not fall into any particular chapter on Project Management.

You're just about through with the book. Congratulations.

*Forrest Wayne Heard*

# Chapter 9

# A Final Look at the 24-month Plan

### The Long-Range Calendar

In preparation for organizing the 24 months of his command, Jackson (the project owner) had the operations officer (the project manager) prepare the paper calendar (scroll) that encircled the classroom used at the offsite. The calendar contained dates of major activities and transition points to focus areas (individual, team, leader, or large unit training). The dates of deployments to New Zealand and the Republic of Korea were plotted. Large scale live fire exercises involving aircraft, artillery, tanks, along with their arsenal of Infantry weapons were displayed.

The timeline, depicted along the top border of the paper, was segmented by quarters represented by heavy vertical lines; months separated by narrow, less prominent vertical lines; and weeks by hash marks along the timeline.

The Army schedules training and operations by fiscal year and numbers the weeks. Week one is the week in which October 1 falls. (October 1, being the first day of the fiscal year.) In directing professional development, classes for the officers fell on the even weeks and those of the NCOs fell on the odd weeks; every leader understood the reference.

The higher headquarters (25th Infantry Division) would rotate the priority for resources (ranges, training areas, helicopter support, etc.) to units based on a six or nine-week cycle. If your unit was in Green cycle, you had priority of resources and you were expected to focus your activities on intensive (large unit) training.

When in Red cycle, your outfit would pull guard duty and fatigue details necessary for keeping the base operating smoothly.

If assigned Yellow cycle, your unit would be the ready brigade, or ready battalion. If war was declared or there was a natural disaster, this unit would be the first to deploy, followed in quick succession by the other battalions. Yellow cycle would logically follow a Green cycle because this unit was the most recently trained on large scale operations.

These cycles were already represented on the battalion's calendar. The company commanders and senior staff officers could easily determine when to schedule large scale training events, and when the organization would be confined to the local area for guard duty. No one expected to conduct much training during a Red cycle. Jackson, being the more innovative manager, had other ideas.

## Red Cycle

Historically, when a battalion landed on Red cycle the details were evenly distributed across the companies so no one company had to shoulder the entire burden. Not so with Jackson. He adjusted their paradigm.

Jackson would assign priorities, within the cycle, to each company. If you were priority 3, your company handled 100% of guard duty requirements and details, like cutting the grass and picking up litter, until you were completely tapped out - no available personnel remained. Priority 2 Company begins taking on tasking after the priority 3 Company could handle no more. Until then, the Priority 2 Company participated in training.

The company designated priority 1 for that week, was fenced from all details until both companies designated priority 3 and 2 were no longer capable of fulfilling the requirements. It was rare that more than two companies' worth of personnel were required.

As a result of this innovative approach, even when his battalion was in Red cycle, each company usually had two or more weeks of uninterrupted training during the 6 week cycle. Due to limited training resources available to the Red cycle units, training was focused on small unit tactics and individual skills.

This discussion sets the stage for you, as you review the calendar posted along the walls, and the two lists available for review—Jackson's professional development topics, and the equipment list.

The operations officer reviewed the highlights of the unit's performance in the latest tactical and administrative evaluations developing a shared knowledge of the unit's recent history, strengths, and *areas for improvement*.

The property book officer (supply officer) reviewed the equipment list from which the company commanders would select the weekly maintenance training. A list of tactical level (weapons and tactics) professional development topics was available, coupled with Jackson's list of educational topics formulated to add arrows to everyone's professional quivers as leaders.

## Planning and Scheduling the Next 24 Months

From these lists, informed by the most recent evaluations, the company commanders selected equipment and professional development topics scheduling them on this calendar, for the next 104 weeks (2 years).

The information contained in the finished product—the scroll—was captured in an annual guidance document and supplemented by quarterly guidance (published one quarter in advance of execution). These quarterly guidance documents and Monday morning training meetings governed the weekly training plan (approved during the one-on-one meetings with Jackson). Each company's training plan was due at least 4 weeks in advance of the respective week.

## Consider the Impact

Over the 12 months that followed this offsite, the officers in Jackson's battalion participated in 24 professional development classes (of 2 hours each); 52 maintenance classes (of ½ hour to an hour); and a handful of model unit training sessions (approximately 4 hours each). I dare say they became the most knowledgeable officers on maintenance, organization, executing training, professional development programs, managing meetings and long-range projects; and understanding the interrelationships of systems in place to help manage organizations.

Several months after the initial offsite, Jackson convened another, shorter, offsite. At this meeting his leadership team confirmed the remainder of the current 24-month calendar and planned for the next 6 months. Although Jackson's tenure with the unit was scheduled to end before these events would occur, he dedicated the same energy in setting up his successor for success. He convened still another update, 6 months later.

Even though Jackson would no longer be in charge, he continued to act as if he were the sole proprietor and lifelong senior executive right up until his last day in the job.

One value he expressed in the annual training guidance document—a document he personally authored—resonates. Under the subheading *Training Philosophy*, he wrote **"We must be prepared to go to war tomorrow. Treat each training day as if it is your final day before commitment to combat. It is not enough to train well; we must train on the right missions, the ones we will perform in combat. Train like we are going to war tomorrow; we will someday."** That was certainly how he ran the battalion, and expected his commanders to run their companies.

**Erwin Rommel: The best form of welfare for the troops is first-rate training.**

## What is in store for the next chapter?

You are on the back stretch now and it is important to devote a few pages to communications. In past times, armies in a defense laid telephone wire for communications, and used field telephones (you may have seen them in old WWII movies). The responsibility for laying wire to lower echelons rested with higher. Units on the right, lay wire to units on the left.

In preparing a defense, an organization didn't wait for orders to begin the wire-laying process. It was expected. Nor did you wait for the wire from higher headquarters to arrive at your foxhole before you pushed your team out to your subordinate commands. You didn't wait for the organization on the right to show up before dispatching your wire team to locate and establish communications with the unit to your left.

Communications planning was constant, and the activities to establish and maintain contact were immediate, and ongoing. In addition, if communications were disrupted, there was an established, well-rehearsed, and routinely-tested plan for discovering the root of, and repairing a problem. Teams from both ends of the phone lines would move towards one another looking for the source of the breakdown.

You might find this a pretty good communications plan in many ways. Corporate headquarters or the senior person in the relationship should own the responsibility of ensuring good, amicable communications that builds trust with the subordinate managers, the direct reports.

Midlevel managers can be reluctant to contact a senior several times a week to chat, unless you (the senior leader) have directed him or her to do just that. When there is a disruption of good communications, both sides should work to restore the flow of information.

In the next chapter, you will take a quick look at one-on-one communications with those you evaluate. We will also look at corporate communications as senior executive to connect the enterprise when offices span the country, located in multiple countries or several continents…or your disconnected team is located just down the hallway.

# Chapter 10

# Communications

### Who is responsible for good communications?

Climate surveys are often used to reveal aspects about an organization from the employees' perspectives that may be unknown to the senior management team. In one organization, a climate survey conducted by the previous senior executive indicated the employees were dissatisfied by several aspects of communications within the corporation.

It was suggested to the incoming senior executive that, with an organization as far flung as the one he was taking over he could not over-communicate. Offices away from the headquarters—satellite sites—had been routinely surprised by learning, late in the game, of important ongoing initiatives, or cancellations of projects that were still being actively supported. Surprisingly, personnel at the satellite office never heard from him again during the year he occupied the seat. Climate surveys are worthless if issues are not actioned or at least investigated.

The Captain played by Strother Martin in *Cool Hand Luke*: **What we've got here is failure to communicate.**

Returning to the point made at the end of Chapter 9, and in the discussion regarding responsibility, the senior executive is responsible for everything the organization does or fails to do...and that includes effective communications.

Drucker. "**The second thing to do to manage oneself and to become effective is to take responsibility for communications.**"

In his book *Management*, Drucker devotes a chapter to Managerial Communications. He reminds you to use carpenter metaphors when talking with carpenters.

## One-on-one communications with your Direct Reports

One of the most important responsibilities senior executives fulfill is that of clearly defining and agreeing on the values, behaviors, and objectives of their direct reports.

In the discussion of the method Jackson established, you may recall he required each direct report to develop a list of annual objectives, both personal and for the office. This meeting took place almost immediately upon arrival. Jackson would review every objective. He would direct some to be reordered, to show prioritization; he would suggest others to be added. Jackson would require a rewrite of all objectives, adding the phrase *as indicated by* followed by an objective metric from which to gauge success.

It became a monthly routine to meet with Jackson to discuss progress, reorder priorities, or discuss plans for achieving one, or several, of the objectives for the year.

Performance counseling is significantly less anxiety ridden when the senior executive conducts routine, scheduled meetings throughout the performance period.

If, on the other hand, you get an e-mail or phone call from your rater that suggests meeting for a performance counseling, and it's not time for your annual review, you might jump to the conclusion, *it's time to update the resume.* You worry. Your employment with the company might be coming to an end.

With Jackson, meetings for performance counseling were an ongoing process of developing you into a seasoned professional. His meetings were also an example of how leaders should be developing their teams through routine coaching.

## Capturing Performance for Counseling and Evaluation

A method used in the Army for jotting down information for use in performance counseling, and evaluations, is the STAR (Situation, Task, Action, and Result) Process. It's proven to be an effective way to capture information about performance and context. It can be used by the rater, or it can be used by someone else in a leadership role to provide input to a rater.

At ROTC summer camp, the tactical officers (mentors to the cadets) would describe a situation in which the cadet was engaged. For example, 'the organization was involved in tactical training in a field environment' or was 'conducting marksmanship training with their rifles.'

After setting the stage, they would discuss the task given to the cadet, such as 'organize the platoon for an ambush patrol', or 'organize the ammunition issue point, at the rifle range.' This was generally the shortest of the STAR entries.

In the next box, the tac officer would describe what actions the cadet undertook, or failed to take, in executing the task. One might describe how the cadet invested a few minutes thinking about the task before issuing orders. If tasks were delegated, or counsel sought with other members of the leadership team, before calling the platoon together, those actions were also noted. The evaluator would observe and record as many key actions as possible.

Rounding out the STAR report is a narrative of results, such as 'the platoon was prepared to load the trucks on time and arrived at the rifle range with all equipment.'

The STAR format, in abbreviated form, can be useful for jotting down observations on 3X5 cards, as you are making your daily visits to the production line, or meeting with members of your management team. Usually, the spot report is limited to one specific action, as a reminder to you of the actions taken by the employee, or when an employee failed to take action, but should have. The 3X5 cards are reviewed as you prepare for upcoming performance counseling.

This technique of observing, note taking, and filing for review, also backs up your evaluations with specific examples and dates. Instead of relying on your memory or reporting "John did a really good job", you have hard (specific) data to report. "On Jun 1, during the morning maintenance inspection, John noticed the chain guard was missing. He 'pulled the Andon cord' and stopped unsafe operations, possibly saving life or limb."

One last comment about talking with members of your team; Use your time with employees to build people up. If you need to make a correction, find a way to do it in the most acceptable, and effective way.

It's better to handle corrections of rank-and-file employees or members of someone else's team, through your direct reports whenever possible. Of course, safety issues demand immediate attention. There is an old saying that inappropriate behavior you don't *correct*, you *condone*. That's true even if you really think the behavior is appalling and you intend to say something about it to their supervisor. Everyone knows you saw it, but you didn't correct it. To the audience, that means you're okay with it. Don't let that misunderstanding have a chance to grow legs.

## A Senior Leader Making Corrections

One Saturday morning, at Fort Bragg, several recent graduates of jump school—the paratrooper qualification course—dressed in civilian attire, crossed paths with Lieutenant Colonel Donald Williford, their new battalion commander.

LTC Williford asked if they had any issues settling into life in the 82nd Airborne Division. He asked about their platoon sergeants and platoon leaders. Had the young Troopers written home and informed the parents of their new addresses? Were they getting enough to eat? How was the quality of food in the mess hall? He asked about their hometowns. It was a very pleasant conversation.

Before they parted ways, he added, "Oh, by the way, in the 82nd we salute even when we are in civilian clothes, as a greeting and a sign of camaraderie between fellow paratroopers. So, make sure you do that, even on Saturdays." He didn't say it in a severe way. The information was transmitted from one professional to another.

Although the young Troopers had not saluted when they first encountered him, they did as he left. He returned their salutes and continued on his way towards the mess hall; to check on the quality of breakfast that Saturday morning.

Drucker advises the commander must eat the soup from the same pot as the company. To understand how well the soldiers are fed, a leader must often forego the food served at their home to eat with the troops...even when it is inconvenient, (Or especially when it is inconvenient). As Jackson would say, **"Food is part of the soldier's pay."**

It was only in reflection the young troopers realized they just received an a** chewing for the infraction of not saluting. LTC Williford had stopped, not just to chat with them but to correct their behavior—failure to salute. Certainly, the conversation would have been more succinct with someone who had been in uniform a few more days than these young soldiers. LTC Williford was a class act.

## Mass Communications

One-on-one communications during performance reviews with your direct reports, and conversations you have when out of the office, talking with your assembly line or loading dock personnel are just one category of your communications responsibilities. In this section, the importance of communication in a systematic, routine way to the corporation, or your division at large, will be addressed.

Communications is a tricky business.

Consider the situation: You convene a stand up meeting every morning. You discuss key activities; you reinforce corporate values, routinely. Instead of being a hoarder of information, you freely share it.

But a climate survey reflects most personnel in your division consider communication to be one of the biggest deficiencies in your organization. You cannot believe it. How could they be so wrong? Yes, how could THEY have gotten it so wrong?

A planning and oversight team once found itself outgrowing their original office space. The scope of the job and the number of personnel assigned had increased. They arranged an additional office space in the same building and adjusted their seating arrangements. The displaced members of the team were merely a short walk down the hallway from the main office. All the team members got along well. They had a great boss, who was respected by every team member.

Even with all these positives, communications would often fail. Occasionally, the office where the senior manager sat, would distribute an office email 'reminding' the team of an upcoming event. The event that was old news to members of one office was, in fact, an initial announcement to the displaced team members in the other office. The conversation about the event in the other office had been robust; everyone participated. Memories of the personnel in that office suggested everyone in the organization must be aware of it but unfortunately, that wasn't always the case.

In another office, the senior executive would ensure notes were taken at every meeting, and summaries and decisions published, immediately. If an important conversation was developing, this executive would call for those in other offices to attend, or identify a scribe to take notes so he could ensure other members of his team were updated. Publishing hard copy documents ensures memories remain accurate. As Brian Tracy advises, **"It's not only a good idea to think on paper, it also helps to remember on paper."**

As a leader and senior executive, make it a habit to share information and touch base with everyone in your division. Also eliminate the miscommunications that occur, especially when your team is occupying more floor space than your own living room. Every room away from yours increases the problems in communication. If you occupy several floors of a building, your communications problems increase, again.

Additional buildings? More complex problems. Satellite offices in different states, countries, or continents? Even more complex communications requirements. Spread your enterprise around the world, with various communication methods, and your problems become legion.

If you haven't discovered a method of defeating the band of inhibitors, or you haven't developed a method for keeping your team (all your team) informed, expect problems. If you only communicate when you need something and you rarely venture outside your office don't expect much dedication to your initiatives. You may get compliance, but not commitment.

In *Who Says Elephants Can't Dance?*, Bill Gerstner describes how he went to great lengths to ensure the word was getting to the entire population of employees using the in-house e-mail system. Of course, at his level he also had constituencies to address on Wall Street, in the corps of retired IBMers, stockholders, and on his board.

In the past, announcements and policies were posted onto bulletin boards and managers were required to pass along information. In today's digital environment, employees should be better informed but the reality doesn't seem to corroborate this. Can it be the ubiquitous nature of available information has lulled managers into thinking they are no longer responsible for ensuring information flow? Are you falling into the trap of on-line leadership or management?

You may think if the information is available, people must be well informed. That's a bad assumption.

If you are going to post all the news on your office website, then you must reinforce to your team their requirement to read it daily. It must become habitual for everyone, and you must continue to reinforce the practice. Remember Rickover's enjoiner for *'courageous patience'*. You must occasionally send out a message via personal email to "check today's board for the announcement…or requirement for…" You can't leave communications to chance.

As the senior executive you should take time weekly, or even daily, to send a message to your team…those who aren't occupying the same office spaces. The outliers should be getting the same information you are sharing, or you've heard shared at your office, corporate headquarters.

You should also make provisions for getting unfiltered information from the rank and file. If you don't take pains to develop a process to gather information, you will rarely stumble over it in the course of your day.

Drucker may have said it best when he spoke of the leader who goes out to see for himself, **"Not that he distrusts the subordinate; he has learned from experience to distrust communications."** I've also heard the same sentiment as, **"I trust my people. I just don't trust communications; mine to them or theirs to me."**

## A Cautionary Tale

Be diligent in ensuring reputations remain intact. It's very easy for the home office to adopt a position on someone who works in a satellite office based on one event, or worse, an incorrect version about the event.

Churchill: **A lie gets halfway around the world before the truth has a chance to get its pants on**.

When it is originally reported at the home office someone stumbled in a task, this news generally gets front page, above-the-fold coverage. When the story is corrected, it usually happens in the Community Section, page 6, at the bottom of the page.

A year later, when the party who was reported to have stumbled, visits the corporate office, he still hears questions about the mishap, from the perspective of the front-page coverage, not the corrected version.

As a leader—the senior executive—you have an obligation to ensure the correct version gets as much play and air time as the original, juicier tale.

## **Communications, a Summary**

Communications in an organization cannot be overemphasized, from leader downward and from the rank and file upward. Gathering the information, and ensuring a conduit upward is often neglected.

The senior executive has the responsibility to ensure the vision and intent are understood; the direct reports receive guidance; and personnel have access to the senior leaders of the organization.

One doesn't have to be a Patrick Henry level orator to influence crowds and have a lasting impact. Thomas Jefferson was said to have a weak, speaking voice. His words are still remembered.

Don't expect too many Pentecostal moments.

A key to effective communications is to take seriously your responsibility to communicate. Counsel and guide your leadership team; spend time daily, talking with those who are doing the work to satisfy customers; and create a conduit for routine information flow through your entire organization. You must also create the process that allows for unvarnished feedback from the organization to you.

In the next chapter, you will again return to the base closure and recapitulate the process of planning and executing the project. For your use, as a template for action, the synopsis will extract the vital steps effective managers employ for ensuring success.

# Chapter 11

# Mission, Vision, Intent

In this chapter, we return to the plan to close the base; simplify the structure for developing a plan and executing a project; and bring together the lessons from preceding chapters. With this executive summary, you should be able to establish a template for actions for your next project.

### Setting the Stage for Successful Mission Analysis

Before the first meeting, the senior executive and the core staff reviewed all the information available about the move from their home base. Colonel Katz, the base commander and project owner, developed his guidance.

Administrative preparation included:

- Creating a large-scale timeline to display on the wall, with specific dates plotted along the timeline, based on preliminary research.

- Identifying scribes.

- Setting up RFI, RFS, RF$ charts to capture the requirements.

- Consolidating the reference materials in which the guidance and specified tasks were recorded.

- Assembling the necessary supplies like maps, easel pads, whiteboards, etc.

## Mission Analysis

### "The after-action report starts now!"

At the initial meeting, the operations officer, a key member of the core staff and project manager, introduced the project and announced the mission.

A mission statement for an operation contains very selective information. In it are the 5 Ws - *who, what, when, where* and *why*, (Summarized as task and purpose). Not included in a mission statement is *how*. This is developed after the analysis.

As the information began to sink in, as to what the staff was going to do, the project owner—Katz—discussed his vision and intent.

Intent is the second part of a mission statement and provides guidance about the overall, desired end state. This knowledge, and understanding, empowers action in the absence of orders.

Lieutenant Colonel (later Colonel) Stan Florer would start every mission analysis by announcing, **"We will be successful when…"** and proceed to describe what he would consider *overwhelming success* from start to finish. He included a statement about safety within his vision and intent discussion.

After the project owner described the vision and intent, the project manager would resume control of the meeting and facilitate the discussion as the project team (the core staff, and senior managers of the outlying operations) conducted the METT-TC analysis.

After the team exhausted the list of specified tasks, each task was reviewed. Every attendee identified the key activities required of his, or her, office generated by that individual task. This examination resulted in a long list of implied tasks. Implied tasks result from planners (subject matter experts) identifying complementary activities based on their knowledge, training, and experience.

The team assigned dates and drew connections between tasks.

At this time, the initial mission analysis was complete.

## Developing and Improving the POA&M

Ultimately, an initial list of activities is developed that is:

- Sequenced

- Identifies completion dates expressed as no-later-than dates

- Designates responsibility

Additional meetings are held with focus groups to understand different perspectives and add activities to the POA&M.

## Developing the Plan

Activities that must be included in the plan are identified in the POA&M. In addition, it is often helpful to prepare a document that discusses the plan expressed in a conversational way. Someone who is not familiar with the planning, or the POA&M, should be able to read the description of the plan and understand what will happen and when major muscle movements will occur.

Think of a POA&M in terms of preflight and in-flight checklists, along with after operations maintenance, with all the incredibly important detail. On the other hand, you may want to describe the plan in terms more like a travel itinerary for general consumption. Include enough detail in the plan to capture important concepts and issues but not so much it is a rewrite of the POA&M.

## Executing the Plan and Managing the Execution

With management activities and in-progress review dates embedded in the POA&M, and the right people on the bus, managing the plan gets easier. Management takes discipline by the project owner to attend every meeting and hold attendees accountable for the activities for which they are responsible.

Meeting discipline and focus is important. Unregulated meetings can bog down, drift, or turn into conversations or philosophy discussions.

Executing includes ensuring the tasks are being done to your standard. That requires inspections. These endeavors require getting out of the office and getting to where the work is done. It also demands your diligence in following up with delegated activities. You must pay the premiums on the insurance policy.

Much of the activity might occur after requests for information (RFIs) are answered. For the base closure team, the main question was, 'Where are we moving?' Until that question was settled, the planning team focused on executing activities on the departure base; and evaluating the available options for their new home and where the training facilities would be available. Throughout the project, they continued to refine the plan.

When a final decision was made about the new location, the team prepared a full court press to investigate, in greater detail the base to which they would move—inspecting the barracks, office spaces, rifle ranges, etc. It was here they hit a snag.

As a result of the Iraqi invasion of Kuwait, the unit at Bad Tölz deployed and was away from Germany for the better part of 6 months. This preempted the scheduled investigation of the other facilities. In like manner, the unit occupying the buildings in which they were to move had also been deployed for combat.

After DESERT STORM had ended and the units redeployed to home station, the move began in earnest. Instead of the orderly approach that had been planned, and inspections of empty buildings to prepare for receiving the new unit. The unit that was scheduled to depart Germany and return to the U.S., was still removing their property from the buildings as the Bad Tölz unit had begun occupying.

One piece of information that must be included to understand the complexity of this project concerns the overall responsibility placed on Colonel Katz. The unit that deployed for combat, and was required to move into the buildings being vacated by the unit returning to the U.S.—1st Battalion 10th Special Forces Group—was just one of several tenant units on the base that was closed—Flint Kaserne, in Bad Tölz. All units assigned to Flint Kaserne moved to different locations. Katz had to replicate this effort for every unit headquartered at Flint.

Ensuring each activity identified in the early phase of planning was executed on time, along with the requirements that surfaced during later phases, were keys to the successful management of the project(s).

*Management by walking around* exercised by the senior leaders provided the rank-and-file members of the organization access to the leadership team. Their routine presence allowed the junior personnel and midlevel managers to pose questions and make suggestions.

By visiting with and talking with those who are doing the heavy lifting, you show appreciation for their work and become aware of their issues.

One habit you may find useful is to carry a pen and notepad (or an electronic version), at all times. When someone offers a tip or suggestion, or asks a question you aren't prepared to answer, write it down and follow up as soon as possible. Remember Jackson's advice regarding a short pencil.

Besides freeing your mind from remembering small details, documenting a suggestion or question has another surprising effect. It shows respect to the person who has provided the suggestion or asked the question.

In Chapter 12, you will read of a meeting convened to garner support for a political candidate. A D.C. team for a presidential hopeful was in town to meet with former business executives and retired military leaders residing in the state. These retired executives arrived with several good ideas based on their experience and familiarity with the local political landscape. The candidate's team made a serious faux pas. In the next chapter, you will bear witness to this stumble and one retired executive's response after the D.C. team left. You don't want your employees to walk away from an interaction with you with this executive's perception.

Embed the lessons-learned activities into the POA&M and begin collecting observations immediately.

As the project owner, commit to attend every status meeting. If there is another meeting that conflicts with the in-progress review change it, or change the project status meeting to eliminate the conflict. For the energy levels to stay high, you must convene and attend the meetings. The attendees are reporting to you. Accept no late task completions that haven't already been discussed.

Meet more often as the completion date grows closer. Manage short falls and emergencies quickly. Have a plan to provide overwhelming capability to any issue that confronts the team and endeavors to delay an activity in your project. In Stray Voltage, you will be introduced to one unit's combat SOP to ensure overwhelming success (or forestall a disaster) that can be used to ensure success in a corporate setting, if applied.

Remember, this may be only one of several projects for which you are responsible. Like Meloy, you must be active in all initiatives, projects, and daily operations, meeting with as many of those involved as you can, as often as you can. Very few activities in the workplace are more effective in building team consciousness, cohesion, and commitment to excellence than personal visits and genuine interest, by senior leadership, in the employees and their families. These are the ones on your side of the lever and will determine how far you will move the earth—your ultimate success.

## Post-execution Activities

After you've executed every activity, and the project is complete, convene the after-action review. Collect the data immediately, while memories are fresh; before urgent events overtake the team. Identify the lessons and how you are going to take action on them. Adjust your policies, practices, and procedures. Establish suspense dates for completing the actions.

Develop the D-day calendar.

Publish the after-action report (AAR). Spur team members to read the AAR by asking about the contents during future meetings.

In the final chapter, there are insights into effective executive-level behavior, and tips on various aspects of project management and problem solving. If you are facing a problem, develop a solution. Included will be suggestions that can be particularly helpful if you are serving as the senior executive or business owner.

# Part III

There is only one chapter in Part III. In it, you will find vignettes that do not fit neatly in the other chapters. These ideas and insights are grouped into Chapter 12 as **Stray Voltage** or **Bon Mots**.

# Chapter 12

# Stray Voltage

This chapter contains parting shots that should prove helpful as you transition to, or begin working with, senior management. There will be a few suggested Dos and a few cautionary Don'ts. None will be absolutes. These snippets are reported as tightly as possible while keeping their effectiveness, and understanding intact. One sage advised the **key to good writing is not to write so that an idea can be understood, but to write in a way the message can't be misunderstood**.

The suggestion goes hand in hand with the Broadway tradition that says **amateurs practice until they can get it right; professionals practice until they can't get it wrong**.

These narratives are not in any particular order, nor do they, in most cases, build onto one another.

### Management

### Bowling Management

A consultant friend of mine describes some management techniques as bowling with a black curtain between the bowler and the pins. The curtain is halfway down the lane. A manager peaks around the curtain and tells you what your score was a few frames ago but you are never told where the ball is hitting. You are, too often, looking in the past and can't impact 'now' or the next release.

### Recommendation

Adopt a system that reflects where your ball is hitting, right now, and how to correct the release for a strike.

Dr. W. Edwards Deming in his 14 points: "**Build quality into a product throughout production.**"

Or as Harold S. Dodge opined: **"You cannot inspect quality into a product."**

## Shortstop the Shortfalls; Manage for Overwhelming Success

The 1st Cavalry Division, the unit featured in the book and movie "We Were Soldiers Once and Young" had a response protocol based on *half an hour*. If a small unit (squad or platoon) got into a scrap and couldn't resolve the situation within 30 minutes, the next higher-level organization (company) was inserted into the equation (airlifted or walked in).

After this additional firepower had an opportunity to settle the affair but hadn't, after half an hour, a battalion was moved in, and so on until there was absolute success. The leaders piled on assets and capability.

Unlike sales and marketing, or production management, failure in battle meant wounds and death. Senior leaders ensured through proven processes, and actively managing the fight, the organizations below them had a maximum opportunity of success.

Can you adopt something similar in a factory? Have you heard of a situation in which a plant manager, or division head is informed 'if things aren't turned around, within the year, senior management will close the plant?"

If your corporation has a plant that is succeeding somewhere, then someone must have figured it out. That's not a secret you want to keep. Start ensuring success. Pile on the assets, to include knowledge and insights to faltering operations. Don't issue the challenge (threat) without piling on the assets and capability. Don't wait for failure. Manage for overwhelming success.

## Have a problem? Develop a process.

A young lieutenant had finished his tour of duty with the military and had been hired by a corporation to fix their parts supply warehouse operations. In one of his first boardroom meetings, the senior managers began to lament another problem that had been plaguing their operations. The former lieutenant listened intently and asked how long they had been aware of the problem. 'Several years' was the response. He naively asked, "Isn't that long enough to have figured out how to fix it?"

It was, of course, long enough but sometimes management teams 'fall in love' with the problem, and not in finding a solution. They almost always dislike having the youngest member of the team point out the emperor has no clothes.

If you discover a problem, then develop a process to solve it.

Drucker writes about the recurring crisis in *Management*. **"If a crisis happens - the first time it happens, one fixes it. But if it happens again, then one finds out the cause and fixes it so the crisis never happens again."**

## Cold Calls and Good Ideas

One distraction many small businesses, and local offices of big corporations, report is the disruption created by cold calls from sales representatives seeking appointments.

Taking the challenge, *if you have a problem, develop a process*, the local office examined the situation. The management team didn't like interruptions, but they also counted on the people living in the community, including the sales representatives, to buy their products. In addition, the way the U.S. economy works is often salespeople are the bringers of good ideas and solutions to problems you have, or might face soon.

Some of these problems will be revealed too late to prevent, unless the sales representative alerts the business owner or corporate office to the potential.

The two halves of the problem: You do not want interruptions of your personal calendars, but you don't want the good ideas to slip by you, or fail to discover hidden problems before they surface.

You also want to avoid the problem of choosing a company with which to partner only to discover later it doesn't provide a high-quality product. Sometimes that can happen when the local executive has just completed a major project and the cold call salesman happens to show up at the right time. The salesman is ushered into the decision-maker's office. The decision maker is in a good mood; likes the offering; and says "Yes" only to find out later, it wasn't a well-researched decision.

Ending the cold calls and snap decisions was really a simple solution after the company put their minds to it. Instead of lamenting a problem, they chose to solve it.

## The Solution

When a sales person called (in person or on the phone), the gatekeeper referred them to the *process* that explained how to gain an audience with the decision makers. The sales rep had until the 15th of the month to submit an idea (feature and benefit) for review, using a structured concept paper. The idea was evaluated to determine if the committee, established to review good ideas, and the primary user would be interested in listening to a presentation.

Sales personnel representing ideas that had generated interest among the reviewing team were notified that on the last working day of the month, at 9 am, the Good Idea Review committee would meet. The presenter would have 15 minutes to convince the committee the idea was worth evaluating further. From this audition, the sales representative gained an appointment with a decision maker during the next month.

Adopting this process, or one of your own design, eliminates your interruptions while ensuring you have the best opportunity to hear about the latest gadgets, doodads, software, product offerings, or benefit programs. You schedule the Good Idea Review committee once a month (or quarter) where you focus your efforts as a team on the ideas or products presented.

There is also a great benefit in implementing this system to those who are in sales. They aren't wasting their time calling on people who aren't interested or can't use the product or service.

## Taking over a Project Midstream

Hopefully, you won't fall behind on a major project and get a visit by a no-nonsense consultant like turnaround guru, D. Vader.

As you may remember, the Death Star project manager, Moff Jerjerrod, in George Lucas's *Return of the Jedi*, fell behind in his project. He greeted his surprise guest warmly (fearfully) only to be rebuffed with, **"You may dispense with the pleasantries, Commander. I'm here to put you back on schedule."**

On a serious note, you may be called upon to take over a project that has already begun. A project owner or manager has departed. In long term projects, you might take over a project, serve as a project manager, and move on before the project is complete. Government acquisition programs often have long lead times.

What if you discover the project for which you have been given responsibility isn't going to fulfill expectations of the customers? What if you roll out the product with great fanfare, and the customers aren't impressed?

One project manager was confronted with this situation. He went headfirst into the project with the understanding (and expectation) the imminent product roll-out would result in universal praise, and accolades. He was shocked when the customers looked at the result and proclaimed, "That's an ugly baby." After defending it, unsuccessfully, in the pre-rollout meeting, he fell back and regrouped.

The project manager acted in a way his predecessor had not. He convened a meeting of the customers and brainstormed the desired solution. He adjusted the delivery date and mounted as much 'chrome' as possible to satisfy the client. He threw in additional 'undercoating'. After achieving satisfactory support for the product, he spent the remainder of his time as project manager adjusting the product so it resembled the product the customers had expected.

In sales, one must occasionally (routinely) resale the product before a final decision on the purchase, again while awaiting the delivery, and often once again after the product has been delivered.

(In this instance, you can use the broad definition of sales that suggests sales is the process of transferring enthusiasm for a product, service, or idea from one to another.)

Statesmen must (should) continually sell their ideas even after they are accepted, and their change team is elected. They must keep reminding constituents, this is why we chose this path. This is why you supported our position.

Don't begin to believe your supporters no longer need to hear why your position is valid.

Don't fall into the all-too-common belief your constituents and customers still appreciate the fine points of your program or the product they bought. You must sell them on your ideas routinely.

Parents are continuously selling the idea of their values to their children.

When you stop selling your ideals, others will start making cold calls on your children, customers, and constituents, to sell their values, products, and ideas.

## Business and Bureaucracy- Approaches to building a baseball team.

Imagine you reside in a town at the turn of the 19th to the 20th century and you want to develop a professional baseball team. Living in this town are two incredibly gifted players who regularly practice together. Either one could hold any position on a pro team but one is particularly gifted as a pitcher; the other as a catcher.

Both can field a ball, run the bases, throw, and bat with distinction. They are interested in serving as the nucleus of a ball club.

What would your next steps be in fielding a team to play against other teams that are organizing around the state?

Perhaps you will want to recruit a first baseman or shortstop. Maybe you want to hire an outfielder. You begin considering who could serve as the player coach. Cross training someone to serve as the third base coach might be a technique you select.

If you own a business (or a baseball team) each person you hire must contribute to the bottom line in a significant way. Wouldn't you agree?

On the other hand, how would a bureaucracy organize for a baseball team, given the same conditions at the beginning…an excellent pitcher and catcher?

A bureaucracy would probably elevate someone to manage the team, immediately. This person might not (probably won't) have the subject matter expertise in the skill sets you revere in a baseball club. However, this manager has worked in the organization long enough for the next promotion, or deserves another chance to develop as a manager. Or, worse, if the idea of starting a ball team is not particularly well supported, a skillful bureaucrat may farm out a less talented, disruptive manager as the coach.

Employees will know, immediately, how much value you place on the initiative based on who you select to lead it.

**Drucker: "No matter how hard managers try to keep their decisions a secret - and some still try very hard - people decisions cannot be hidden. They are eminently visible."**

The newly assigned manager will have the two ball players identify the skill sets—run, hit, catch, field, throw, play as part of a team. The bureaucrat will identify a need for a coach (midlevel manager) in each skill, forming functional (or…more probably dysfunctional) teams. Again, these coaches won't necessarily be hired for their skills in playing ball but the manager needs to have another level of management between himself and the players. About this time, you have about 7 to 9 persons on the payroll but still only two ball players.

In reality, mature teams may hire coaches to help with these skills, but rest assured each will be skilled in the activity they are hired to coach, and in the coaching of those skills. Hiring the coaches will come after the players' roster has been filled. The manager will be hired to remove, not add to, the burden of administering the team, so the players can concentrate on playing ball.

## Back to the Bureaucracy

The head coach in the bureaucracy hires coaches who are often friends and have similar managerial talent. The bureaucracy's head coach begins to build an empire. Those who are hired, are beholden to him, and will support his suggestions readily.

The managers (senior and functional skill coaches) will begin to discuss who they should hire to complete the team. The suggestions of the catcher and pitcher, who play ball with all the local players, will often be ignored.

The managers will soon notice the catcher and pitcher are way too chummy. They are always talking about baseball. When other ball players call the office to ask about the team, they only want to speak with one of these two players. The head coach separates the two, assigning each to different coaches…one who can't throw a strike and the other who can't catch one.

Eventually, the catcher and pitcher will grow frustrated and move on to another team. The roster will be filled with the mediocre and coached by the inadequate. The managers will update their resumes showing they were coaches, for one year, responsible for standing up a ball team from scratch. They will go on to be hired by other bureaucracies that want to field a ball team and need experienced coaches to run the program.

This story probably sounds ridiculous to you but this is exactly how one organization filled an office in which expertise and manpower was needed. Some might say, the office was a much more important field of endeavor than even baseball.

When the original, creative leader of this shop departed due to promotion, a newly-assigned senior executive (who wasn't interested in this aspect of the portfolio) selected a replacement manager who was not particularly well suited for the job.

**Drucker: "Executives who do not make the effort to get their people decisions right do more than risk poor performance. They risk losing their organization's respect."**

This manager brought in a team of similarly suited friends who had no expertise in the mission. Not surprisingly, their office managers had eagerly approved their departures. The work stations of the two subject matter experts were separated where the experts could be supervised by the new management team. Shortly, thereafter the subject matter experts departed.

Fight the urge to assign managers who aren't experts, or who don't at least have a working knowledge of the activities they will manage. Look for mangers who know how to use knowledge workers.

## Good for the organization or building an empire?

There can be times when you, as the senior executive, are presented with an idea that seems well reasoned and might be a good thing for the organization, but you suspect that the advocate might also be trying to build an empire.

The advocate comes to you with a plan to consolidate one activity with another and elevate one deserving person to manage both activities to ensure synchronization. Without being offensively obvious that he expects to head the new structure, the advocate describes what he considers to be the qualifications for the best candidate, which sounds a lot like his or her resume. This should be a tipoff.

An easy way to expose the politics, or confirm the sincerity, is to ask the advocate to brief it again (immediately or within a few days). Convene the meeting after you've invited someone else to the meeting…someone who could also be a likely candidate for the position.

Throughout the second briefing, turn to the rival asking for her thoughts about the initiative. Do you see the advocate showing the same level of enthusiasm during the second briefing when he discovers he might be selling the idea to his competition, and possibly his new boss?

Drucker warns against creating a job for a person. **"If the job is designed for an individual rather than for a task, then it has to be restructured every time there is a change in the incumbent. And, as experienced managers know, one cannot restructure one job. There is a true "domino effect", a true chain reaction. Restructuring a job usually means restructuring a score of jobs, moving people around, and upsetting everybody. And for this reason, jobs have to be designed to fit a task, rather than a particular person."**

<u>Gut genug? Die Kunde entscheidet.</u>

Good enough? The customer decides.

One of the most effective means at your disposal to discover what your customers or clients feel about your corporation, and to gather suggestions for improvement, is the Customer Satisfaction Survey. Several large airline and hotel chains and a few on-line businesses administer first-rate customer comment programs.

When one submits a comment or complaint to one of those corporations, there is an immediate response that alerts you the message has been received. A follow-up message arrives soon thereafter that is personal in nature and proves the concern or accolade has actually been read.

For providing specific feedback, the customer may be offered additional rewards points for hotel upgrades, or a voucher to use on the next flight.

Imagine the helpful information corporations could gather if they included this question with their surveys, or included them on survey cards located in the seat back in front of you on your next flight. *What must we do to satisfy you when flying with us? What are the small ways we could increase passenger enjoyment, from your perspective?* Instead of guessing what actions to take, with this targeted crowd-sourcing you may be able to create a reservoir of good ideas from your customers.

In management books and studies, one can find examples of proactive management activities resulting from surveys and help desk reports. Some companies make it a requirement for management to take turns on the 'help desk floor' responding to customer concerns. Not satisfied with written, unemotional, sanitized reports, these managers get the full force of the emotion that is tied up in the event. As they take the brunt of the verbal assault of a dissatisfied customer.

## Restaurant Customer Survey

There is one semi-fast-food restaurant that seems to have a great plan to garner suggestions and ratings of service. On each receipt is a phone number and a website, along with a request to rate the service, quality of food, and the facility. Responding to the survey, by phone or on-line, automatically enters the patron into a monthly drawing for a substantial cash prize.

One frequent customer would complete a survey after every visit, routinely identifying crew members, by name, who were performing in an outstanding manner at the register, kitchen, or dining area. 'This crew member was friendly and helped an elderly patron'. Another was 'always busy clearing the tables for customers.' One in particular was 'great at the cash register.'

To help you visualize the store arrangement: There were several cash registers at the front counter.

The customer reported that one team member would consistently scan the crowd looking for the person reticent about moving to the cash register to place an order. Standing tall (she never slouched or leaned on a register), this employee would invite the customer to her register.

Looking the customer in the eyes, she would smile, greet them and ask for the order. If the customer was hesitant, she might offer suggestions. After they ordered, she would instruct them about their options. She never used youthful jargon on older customers. She was the model of what the corporation or franchise should seek when recruiting, hiring, training, and retaining personnel at the point of sale.

Using the corporation's survey and customer comment system, the frequent diner suggested that local managers observe her, to feel for what he, a loyal patron, considered perfection in the customer service realm at the front counter. He asked them to call so he could provide a more complete description of what he had observed.

He also shared a frustrating flaw in their restaurant setup, a flaw that could easily be corrected. Customers, especially repeat customers, would form a queue behind one person waiting for one of the registers to become free. On occasion, the line would be quite long. Often, when a new customer entered the restaurant and observed only one person at a register placing an order, the customer would walk directly to the register, not seeing there was already a queue. The burden of making a correction rested on the people standing in line.

The frequent customer suggested that store managers prepare a sign - LINE FORMS HERE. This would mitigate the problem of unobservant customers not seeing the line for service. A corporation shouldn't leave it to customers to inform other customers of the protocols. The customer asked the company to call for a more complete description of his recommendation.

If management had researched his customer rewards number, they would quickly discover this customer ate at their restaurants several times a week.

The customer began adding "Please call me" on each survey. Unfortunately, no one ever called. That's right, no one ever called.

In conversations with several restaurant team members—ones who had been mentioned favorably by name in surveys—he never found one whose outstanding performance had been commended by management because of the survey results. How sad. Management had a golden opportunity to reinforce great customer service but failed to take advantage of their (probably very expensive) customer feedback system.

Advice: Establish a system that embraces the positive attributes of the large hotel and airline chain customer survey systems. Use your customer response system effectively to improve and reward. If a customer wants to take the time to give you counsel, take advantage of the opportunity.

Good enough? The customer will decide.

## Team Plus Up versus Skilled Labor

If you work on projects on which you are routinely or even occasionally assigned part-time help who aren't skilled in your processes, you face a dilemma. The new team members are from different departments or disciplines, but they are yours to employ for a period of time. You may feel it is more trouble to work with the unskilled as it is to go with a leaner, but skilled team.

Consider this solution. Look at the tasks you must complete in the project. Identify the least skill-intensive activities. Or identify all the activities and rank them in order of skill requirements.

Develop an orientation and training program. Gather a list of the talents and interests of your temporary team members. Provide the new personnel an overview of your processes.

Decide if it is better to use your additional work force as an individual team or to spread their talents among your seasoned team members.

Break them in with smaller jobs. Incorporate them completely into your team so they don't feel the 'us versus them' isolation of a new person. This is a leader's responsibility. (See the highlights from Colonel Olivero, and Colonel Waters and how they incorporated SMEs into their office structure in **Using Knowledge Workers**.)

## Orienting the New Hires

### At the Corporate Level

Newly trained paratroopers assigned to the 82nd Airborne Division were initially housed in the 82nd Replacement Detachment. During the week in which the troopers awaited assignments, they were shepherded through a process designed to indoctrinate the new paratrooper and create an understanding how fortunate they had been in qualifying to be a member of this elite unit.

- They received a guided tour of the 82nd Museum where they learned of the exploits of Sergeant York in WWI; the heroic WWII combat jumps; and operations around the world. They were introduced to a legacy they were expected to uphold.

- They were welcomed by the Division Commander. In my case, MG Kroesen.

- The Division Command Sergeant Major met with them and discussed the seriousness of their mission and national security.

- The square patch with the double A (signifying the All-American Division) and arching Airborne tab were sewn on the left sleeve of all uniform shirts.

- The Troopers were taken on guided bus tours of Fort Bragg to understand the lay of the land.

- Each Trooper met with a records clerk to confirm the information in their personnel file.

- Each Trooper visited with a finance clerk to ensure the financial records were accurate.

- They were instructed in a few general military subjects and introduced to the chain of command—the military leadership within, and leadership above the 82nd Airborne Division.

- They were counseled and coached on the wearing of the uniform and how to spit shine the jump boots, along with the proper salute of officers assigned to the 82nd, "All the Way, Sir!" or "All the Way, Ma'am!"

Ultimately, after one week of ensuring the new paratroopers were ready to begin work, they were assembled; loaded onto buses with all their personal belongings (in one duffle bag); and were transported to a Brigade.

After a brief welcome by the brigade commander and command sergeant major (CSM), they were marched to a battalion (dragging their duffle bags along). There, they were met by the battalion commander and CSM.

Here, the formation was divided as each Trooper was assigned to a line company for eventual assignment to a platoon, squad, and fire team.

Along this path, every leader met and welcomed the new Trooper. Every sergeant provided counsel for success and warnings for infractions.

Much like the Bible, there seemed to be a lot of "behold" how great it is, and "beware" of not following the rules, as Jim Rohn instructs.

All great companies (corporations) have similar orientations of new employees—flight crews, nurses, front desk personnel, code writers, etc.

You learn the 'regimental history'—the great things your corporation has done in the past, and the vision of what it intends to do in the future.

"This is our history. This is why we are great. This is our vision. This is what we do to make a better community, nation, and world." Like General Electric's "We bring good things to life."

Here are your uniforms. Here are our expectations.

If your organization doesn't have a structured process for orienting new hires, you should consider beginning one.

As you've already seen once in this book: **"You hire qualified applicants. You train good employees."**

## Combat Replacements in the Jungle

Units in combat are routinely "plussed up" with replacements. A first sergeant (1SG) explained his field replacement and orientation system.

When replacements arrived—usually by resupply helicopter—he would write down their names and learn some key facts about each one. What is your skill identifier? (After advanced training, the Army assigns job identifiers to indicate the broad job skill set a soldier has acquired...infantry, armor, supply, finance, etc.) Where are you from and are you married? (The 1SG didn't want the ambush of one platoon to impact one small town in the Midwest with several casualties. Nor did he want to write to two new widows because of one action, if it could be avoided. He spread the married soldiers among the platoons.)

The 1SG would have the replacements spread their ponchos on the ground and dump their rucks (backpacks). He inspected to ensure they had all the required field gear and weren't missing canteens, magazines (the bullet type) and food.

After giving the replacements a quick rundown on the unit's mission, location, and recent actions, he would summon the platoon sergeants to the command post (field headquarters). The platoon sergeants would take the soldiers to platoons where they were to spend the next 12 months...if they were lucky. This process ensured the new guys were fully integrated into their new 'families'.

It helps to develop a system that solves your problems.

## Leadership Tips

### Why senior leaders should say "Not yet" instead of "No"

Often, when an idea is floated in a bureaucracy (private or public enterprise), the default response (when the idea demands resources [and when does it not?]) is "No". Even though the office with responsibility for the action supports this conference, trip, or initiative the answer from cost-conscious senior management is "No".

Let's assume there are four layers of management that must approve the request before substantive action can take place, and the first office has denied the request.

If the event in question is important, the office sponsoring the idea must reserve time on the executive's calendar, explaining why this is important and should be supported to ask the decision be reversed.

If the sponsoring office is successful in their quest, but the second level manager says, "No" the action is returned to the sponsoring office with a non-concur.

This situation demands the originating office convince the first level, again, of the righteousness of their cause and arrange time on the calendar with the second tiered manager who denied the request.

As a request percolates to the final decision maker, every level in between can non-concur, and effectively put an end to the initiative.

As a result of the ponderous approval process, one must convince the first level manager to go to the second level of management and challenge the decision. Gaining an appointment with a busy executive requires gaining access through the gatekeepers to wedge a few minutes into the calendar, to reconsider a decision that has, in this manager's mind, already been made.

Let's assume the team sponsoring the initiative is successful here, but now the third level of management responds with a "No". If the office with the original idea hasn't lost interest, or heart, or they have not missed an important deadline, perhaps they make another run at gaining approval.

First, they must work to get time on the 2nd level manager's calendar. The one who has, most recently, said "Yes" to reexamine the case, to gain her approval, not just for the original idea, but to meet with the 3rd level to present their case.

Again, let's assume they are successful in convincing the most recent non-concur the corporation should fund and support this initiative. The 3rd level manager passes the action to the final authority with a recommendation for approval. The 4th level, the final decision maker at this local headquarters, quickly reviews the request; observes there is a cost involved; and in the austere operating environment, responds with a "No".

At this point, the sponsoring office has a serious decision to make. Is this initiative so important it makes sense to go through all the levels of management to garner support from every manager along the path, to make a last appeal to the senior decision maker?

Will the intermediate managers feel it is worthwhile? Of course, the clock is ticking on the response. Even if successful in gaining approval, will approval come too late to effectively respond? Is the response window still open?

Each office along the way must, again, go through the gatekeepers to find time on the executive's calendar for another conversation. If one of the managers has been called away to corporate headquarters, the action might stop there until she returns.

Gaining approvals at every level above the office at the 'tip of the spear' (closest to the customer) increases time and energy spent by the action office, absorbing precious time from the executives above them. A cumbersome process, like the one I've described, is especially burdensome when the requestor must run the gantlet (or gauntlet, if you prefer) 2 and 3 times for one request.

Even when successful, valuable time could have been used preparing for the conference or trip. And valuable time of the midlevel executives has been wasted, as they review their answers, reconsider the value of the initiative, and recommit to the idea. In some cases, the sponsoring office may have missed an opportunity.

## How do you eliminate this drain on your organization's energy?

## Not Yet!

As a senior executive, how do you eliminate a portion of this wasted time? Instead of responding with an absolute "No", say "Not yet. I need more information." Make "Not

Yet" your default. This simple change eliminates the requirement to convince intermediate managers, or stiffen their backbones, for challenging the senior executive's edict. Instead of a "Non-concur or No", reply with "I can't say Yes based on the information I have." This eliminates the need to get an overriding "Concur" from each department on the way to the senior executive.

You have probably found a "Yes" is much harder to get and every 'No' along the path to a 'Yes' can be a tremendous diversion of energy that could be better spent. As a senior executive, respond with a "Not yet".

## Walk slowly and smile

Somewhere along the way in leader development, you may have been told to walk fast…with a purpose. Successful people walk fast. Adopt a serious look…a war face.

Walking fast with a serious countenance can also make you appear unapproachable. It's easy to misinterpret 'serious' for anger or being upset. Wearing a scowl seems to say, "I'm too busy to talk with you." If the manager is walking briskly with a clipboard or folder in hand, one is less likely to stop him or her for casual conversation…conversation that might reveal issues and build good relationships.

Walk a little slower down the hallways and through the lunchrooms. Look happy to work there and proud to work with the others who work with you. Talk with people. Learn their names.

The Science of People studied successful TED talks. Viewers were asked to rate the speaker on charisma, intelligence, and credibility. They determined 'smiling makes you look smarter'. There were 4 other attributes—among them hand gestures—that correlated with an increase in the number of 'hits'—translated to popularity—on a TED presentation.

## Put a sharp pencil to it

A piece of good advice shared by a retired Lockheed engineer was: **"Put a sharp pencil to it."** Whenever you are facing a problem, especially a financial decision, apply this advice.

Has this ever happened in your hometown? At the beginning of the school year, the local newspaper, on the front page above the fold, reports a shortfall in the operating budget of the county school system. There are insufficient funds to employ a band teacher or other arts-related teacher, or a lacrosse coach or other member of the coaching staff. A hotly-debated bond measure results.

Regardless, if the bond measure fails or succeeds, months later we see in the local paper (far from the front page) a glowing report about members of the school board or county office returning from a successful fact-finding trip to a distant land. Hmmm, you may ask…and should ask…how can we not afford a band teacher but can afford 5 members of the school board to journey to another country to discover how foreign languages are taught. (You may have also noticed that none of the teachers still active in the classroom participated in these fact-finding excursions).

Jim Rohn routinely advised **there is always plenty of money**. It is your philosophy that usually needs to change.

The next time you hear your children's school won't have a band program, or the girl's lacrosse team won't have a coach, ask a few questions. Does the superintendent have an administrative assistant? Does this person earn as much as it would cost for a band teacher or a coach?

In some school systems, the band teacher not only guides the high school band, he also instructs and recruits from all the feeder schools to his high school. On a weekly basis, she may interact with over 200 students.

If one employee (a band teacher) will interact with 200 students and the other employee (the Superintendent's administrative assistant) only supports one person, where are your tax dollars best spent? In some counties, the philosophy might be the students are more important. In others, the administrative offices seem to be most important.

It's not about the money. It's the philosophy.

If that argument is not convincing enough, consider the note that goes out to parents at the beginning of the school year. "Parents, we're counting on you to provide a box of tissue, pencils, pens, sanitary wipes, etc."

Without parental and classroom teacher support, many classrooms would be almost bare except for desks and whiteboards. Ask yourself and the school superintendent this question: "Do the personnel working in the administrative offices (usually more highly paid than the teachers) get similar notes, or is there plenty of copy paper and toner, pens and pencils, and tissue at the central office?

Ask the school board if a committee of parents, teachers, and administrators may look at the budget to see if a creative solution can be found without additional funds, simply shifting money around a bit.

It's almost never about the money. It's the philosophy. So, **put a sharp pencil to it**.

## Phone courtesy

This is an easy fix and shouldn't require discussion, but it does.

If you call someone, identify yourself, by first and last name and your office, slowly. Not all phones are equipped with caller identification. You may not be the only John or Sue who calls this person. Offices are often loud, and the listener might miss your introduction if you rush through it.

If you don't identify yourself, or if you speed through your introduction, acting as if everyone should know who you are, the listener's brain may be busy trying to find clues to your identity instead of listening to your message.

Before you launch into your sales pitch or other soliloquy, ask if you have caught the listener at a good time. Be polite. Ask if you can take a minute of their time, or if you should call back. Don't assume your audience has been sitting idly by the phone all day, awaiting your call. Assume you are interrupting their work. (Don't expect them to be like the Maytag repairman from the old television commercials).

When you call someone for information, don't interrupt them as they are trying to provide it, acting as if you are now in a rush to end the call. After all, you interrupted their day.

One of the reasons Bob Jackson enjoyed so much respect by people throughout the division was his courtesy, to include telephone courtesy. One story told often about Colonel Jackson was a call he made to the 25th Infantry Division headquarters to ask about an upcoming training event.

He reached out to a junior staff officer. Jackson asked about the officer's family; boys' soccer teams; spouse's activities; etc. He showed genuine interest. Jackson asked about their mutual friends from a previous assignment. He allowed the officer to talk without interruption.

As he wrapped up the conversation, Jackson finally got around to asking about the training event. After his questions were answered, he thanked the young officer and told him how much he appreciated the work he was doing. Jackson asked he be remembered to the wife and sons, and then ended the call because he "had a battalion to run."

I can assure you Jackson's time was much more valuable than the young officer's time. Had Jackson called and asked for the information, abruptly, he would have certainly been served with great respect and courtesy. But, because he was also courteous and thoughtful, soldiers lined up to be on his side of the lever.

### Show respect when someone is providing information

This horse has been beaten often enough but you were promised the story earlier in the book.

A presidential campaign season was beginning. A campaign committee from D.C. was coming to the state capital for a meeting with senior executives, business leaders, military leaders, and other influencers from across the state, all of whom were retired. The D.C. team arranged the visit, ostensibly, to gather ideas and garner their support.

The campaign staff began the meeting reciting the great things their candidate would achieve after winning the nomination, and presidency. They discussed the plan for taking each state.

The state influencers began to provide counsel to the young team from Washington. They talked of the issues that concerned the voters in this state. They made practical suggestions for the candidate to earn the nomination. They provided insights and nuance a national level team could not know, but could prove essential to gaining support across the state.

The Washington team enthusiastically thanked the assembly and departed for D.C.

As the assembly departed, one of the more senior executives mentioned what a waste of time this had been. He had traveled on Saturday, forfeiting time with his family and friends. He had plenty to do at home to keep him busy but he had really wanted to support the candidate in his bid.

Another exec asked, "So why do you think it was a waste of time?" His response, "They didn't take a single note." There was no way the information this group of leaders provided would ever be delivered to the committee planning the campaign. The team from D.C. had shown no respect to the leaders who had assembled that Saturday morning. Their failure to take notes indicated to this executive the D.C. team was there only to provide information, not gather it.

Show respect. When someone tries to help you, take notes.

## Activity or the Process

There was a great debate (maybe not great but spirited) among a team developing the education and training program for a new mission which the Army Chief of Staff had expressed a strong interest.

One faction in the debate was adamant individuals and units must receive this education, or undergo this training, before they deployed into combat. This faction felt what was needed was information developed and delivered immediately—information the soldiers could draw upon if they were to find themselves in a particularly dire situation.

The other faction represented the office that developed training products as their profession. Their processes identified the most effective way to deliver every portion of information to develop the necessary skills. It was an elaborate and sometimes effective process.

To this second faction, anything less than a fully examined, extensively debated, professionally prepared program was not, in their opinions, rightly identified as 'training'. Any product produced without the rigor was subpar. The process demanded a year of development. Changes required another year of development.

To those not schooled in the alchemy of training development, it seemed a bit stultified or overly rigid.

A working definition of 'training' might be appropriate at this point. This definition is solely for the understanding within the covers of this book, so you don't have to agree but you'll need to accept it as a position. *Training is the transfer of skills from someone with the skill, to another.*

As a side note, there is a difference between education and training. For some this nuance is difficult to grasp. One of the best ways it has been explained concerns fire and building fires.

Consider the elements of combustion or what is known as the fire triangle—oxygen, heat, and fuel. If an instructor discusses this concept with the class and then provides a practical demonstration of creating fire by rubbing two sticks together, you have been educated.

If your instructor then asks everyone to assemble outside and oversees each individual in rubbing two sticks together until each student can make fire, the instructor has trained you. You have developed the skill. Obviously, there are levels of competence such as the difference between the novice mechanic and the master mechanic.

Steve Crews was an NCO in the 504th Infantry, in the 82nd Airborne Division. He understood training, and how to do it. When a new weapon was fielded, he could develop training on short notice. As a result of his training, the participants could: disassemble and assemble the weapon; conduct a pre-operational check; place the weapon in operation (fire it); take action if it jammed; clear it (make sure it's no longer loaded); and clean it.

He probably knew very little about the bureaucracy of the training process, but if you needed soldiers trained, you could trust he could do it.

Often persons in specialized programs, like training development, become wedded to the process, often to the detriment of the result. Some, unfortunately, may not be good at actual training but are intimately familiar with the process of developing training.

One mentor suggested, about one specific and unnamed, training developer, "**He couldn't train people to pour *water* out of a boot, even if the instructions were written on the bottom of the heel.**" If memory serves, he may not have used the term 'water'…but it was something liquid nonetheless.

If you witness leaders stumped because training developers describe long lead times for developing or changing training, for which the leader is ultimately responsible, caution them to understand there is 'training' and there is the 'bureaucracy of training development'.

## Think on Paper; Remember on Paper

If you are trying to sell someone on an idea, put the idea along with the features and benefits (if appropriate) on paper (or a whiteboard) as you discuss them. Seeing the positives and negatives, versus just hearing them makes the information more concrete and helps prevent the listener from clinging to just one point in the discussion.

If you find yourself in a discussion that seems to be going nowhere and one attendee latches onto a single pro or con, redirect them to the whiteboard. Develop the comparison like sales professionals using the Ben Franklin close. Draw a 'T' and write down the pros on one side and the cons on the other. Putting issues on paper (making it visual) can help develop solutions.

It's helpful if you have already developed a list of pros and cons for the idea. When you present the idea, list the pros and cons you have considered. Invite your antagonist to the board to list others you may have missed. Chances are they won't be able to list many.

With pros and cons listed on the board, start your conversation.

After a meeting, summarize the points that have been agreed upon, or at least what you think everyone has agreed on. Publish the results.

## Reflection

Consider Jackson's battalion management system and how he developed it. The Army has a series of schools in the professional military education system. About every 3 to 5 years, an officer returns to the school system for further, advanced education to prepare them for positions of greater responsibility. All officers attend the same courses along this path.

Unlike most, Jackson must have devoted time to organizing the body of knowledge, by the different systems that were included in the syllabus of his courses. Afterwards, he applied his considerable brain power to the challenge of how to incorporate all the information, the systems, and vital data points into one system of management that ensured excellence in each subsystem.

Perhaps reflection would be a great add-on day to any in-house training course. Enforced reflection—scheduled time—on the subjects the students have been taught.

How would this be done in day-to-day activities? Provide a hand-out to each student that lists the topics on which the instructors provided information. Ask the students to develop a plan that answers this question: How are you going to incorporate the knowledge you acquired here to manage more effectively?

Requiring students to develop their plans increases the learning, much more than if a solution is provided beforehand, even if the school solution is then dissected for full understanding.

The department providing the training could review and publish the best student responses. Perhaps the department could eventually provide a guide that would help managers tie their systems together and elevate the effectiveness of all managers. This change could come about just by mandating something that Jackson probably did on his own, which is reflect on the information and develop a plan to put it to use.

Peter F. Drucker: "**Follow effective action with quiet reflection. From the quiet reflection will come even more effective action.**"

## Out of the box thinking

Ask the right questions in a brainstorming session.

One of the most helpful skills when brainstorming for solutions is to know how to formulate the question. The brain will go to work on any problem you can describe. It will begin generating answers to the question you ask of it. Because of that, it is important to ask the brain the right question. Maybe more important is how to avoid asking the brain the wrong question.

There is a considerable body of knowledge on corporate responses, especially in funding and other support, when an issue is described as a 'problem' and when it is defined as an 'opportunity'. If you are facing one of those situations, you should discover the difference. Defining it one way will garner more resources. Defining it the other will release the creative juices to take advantage of the situation.

## **Asking the right question, (Or asking the question right).**

Consider this situation. You and your spouse are a young couple, and you would like to earn more money. Two of your closest friends, another couple—Tom and Sue—earn significantly more than you, or so it seems. You decide to conduct a brainstorming session on the issue. You craft the question: "Why can't we make as much money as Tom and Sue?" The brain goes to work on the question you've asked. Suddenly, you are overwhelmed with reasons why you can't make as much money as the other couple. Obviously, this is not the right question to ask.

A better question would be: How can we make more money? The brain will work just as hard on this question and provide just as many answers as it would for the "Why can't we..." question.

One of the most creative, out-of-the-box thinkers who managed a new program for the U. S. Army was Colonel Tim Waters.

The Army was facing a dilemma in trying to craft a training program to satisfy a new requirement. The subject matter experts (SMEs) were asking the questions the right way, "how can we... versus why we can't...?" But they weren't coming up with satisfactory solutions.

Tim looked at the problem from a completely different perspective. The SMEs were trying to solve how to develop a training program that would deliver the information in the most effective way. He asked why? They answered his initial question and described how the soldiers would use the information. He again asked, why? Why would they need to know this information? Eventually he helped the SMEs discover that, initially, the Army didn't need to develop a training program; they needed to gather unique information from each soldier. He used the 5Y technique (5 Whys: Ask "Why" 5 times to dig deep into an issue).

The SMEs abandoned the quest for the most sublime training program and developed a software solution to the issue that gathered the unique information, almost effortlessly. Later, they developed an easily understood and deliverable trainer program to support Tim's solution of gathering the unique information.

This was just one instance of his creativity. He showed his staff how to look at a requirement and peel back the layers until you can identify, exactly, what you really need.

In the case described above, the Army needed unique information, not a complex training program built to collect the information.

## Using Knowledge Workers

Peter Drucker coined the term Knowledge Workers in *The Landmarks of Tomorrow* for a growing population of persons with specialized knowledge. Written in 1959, Drucker predicted knowledge workers would be "the most valuable asset of the 21st century institution."

Subject matter experts (SMEs) provide the corporation with technical expertise in an uncommon body of knowledge. Usually in high demand, their knowledge, skills, and abilities are in low density within the enterprise.

Often, they are employed at the highest levels of the organization so their advice provides impact throughout the company. In other cases, they may be installed on a team where the rubber meets the road, at the point of sale.

Two leaders who knew how to get the most from their SMEs and use the knowledge to best advantage were Colonels Olivero and Waters.

These talented managers were responsible for changing the structure of, and developing a new mindset within the U.S. Army in the early days after the 9/11 attack. Taking ownership of the program was in large measure keys to their success.

They included the two SMEs in their office structure and used the knowledge gained from them, in meetings with senior leaders (3- and 4-star Army generals).

Highlights of their technique:

- Incorporated the SMEs into office practices as genuinely valued members of the team. The SMEs were not discriminated against for not being uniformed members of the organization.

- Checked daily for insights into challenges and triumphs, to identify roadblocks and successes. They often asked, "How can I help?"

- Educated the SMEs on the processes and protocols in place, in the large bureaucracy (the Pentagon), and made them aware of the stumbling blocks to creating a new program.

- Assigned experienced staff personnel to assist the SMEs in moving their initiatives through the bureaucracy.

- Included at least one SME in every delegation interacting with General Officers. Before the meeting adjourned, they would ask the SME to correct any misstatements and add any key information that might have been omitted.

- Invested time daily, learning from the SMEs, increasing their personal knowledge of the unique aspects of the program. These daily conversations resulted in these two officers becoming the most knowledgeable leaders in this new program the Chief of Staff of the Army created. This proved very helpful when senior leaders within the DoD asked detailed questions about the mission.

These activities overtly, and subtly, reinforced the value placed on the SMEs' efforts and commitment, not only to the SMEs but also to the other members of the organization.

## Chalk Talks

The Atlanta consultant, referred to occasionally in this book, described a process he called Chalk Talks. When a corporation hired him to teach education and training or coach new leaders, he would begin writing the assigned topic on the board, and asking the attendees what they wanted out of the class. "When we wrap things up 3 hours from now, what information or skill do you want to walk away with as a result of participating in this training? What will make these 3 hours worthwhile to you?"

He would solicit ideas and information from the whole class and write every response on the chalkboard, or whiteboard. When the ideas were exhausted, he reviewed each, agreeing what to cover in training; and occasionally, identified items "we might not get to that, but we can schedule time in a follow-up session on it."

This technique of facilitation engages the attendees, immediately, and helps increase the attention of your attendees throughout the class. By engaging the attendees, you move their minds from their office in-boxes and family concerns, into the classroom.

One CEO in Atlanta—the bench chemist who continued to reinvent himself throughout his career—said of this Atlanta-based consultant, "you leave no fingerprints" when facilitating a brainstorming session.

He meant, as praise, the lieutenant—turned consultant—was able to guide the participants to develop a solution they felt strongly about, and of which they would take ownership.

### If you can tie your shoes, you can learn physics.

This Atlanta-based consultant also worked with the university system in Georgia. Part of his job was to create relationships between the technical colleges and industry. Included in his contract was an opportunity to talk with high school seniors who were on their way to higher education, about succeeding in a university setting.

He entitled his Chalk Talk with these high school seniors, **"If you can tie your shoes, you can learn physics."**

As he stood in front of the assembly of seniors on their way to college, he would ask for a show of hands, "if you can ride a bicycle." Naturally, most hands were raised. (Using a facilitator's technique, he would raise his hand, which seems to encourage a response.) He would acknowledge those who had raised their hands.

He continued and asked about "dribbling a basketball"; "hitting a baseball"; "tying your shoes?" "If you can do those things, or those kinds of things, you can learn physics."

He continued by asking them to think hard about the first time they ever tried to ride a bike, dribble, hit a baseball, or tie their shoelaces. Then he asked, "Were you as good at it the first time, as you are now?"

Of course, they weren't.

"What made the difference?" He would then get the attendees to make suggestions. Their answers usually included: practice and sometimes they would mention coaching. If they had not already identified it, he would suggest there was one more thing as important as practice and coaching—a strong desire to acquire the skill.

He would then relate a story about his struggle in high school with the math courses for college-bound students. It was difficult for him.

After being commissioned as a lieutenant in the Army, he was required to attend a course where he had to calculate the downwind drift of nuclear weapons based on the weapon's yield, and prevailing winds. This was part of his job as a lieutenant, so he strongly desired to learn the subject, and he did so, with no trouble. (And yes…this is the lieutenant who asked the assembled managers, "Isn't this long enough to have developed a solution?")

He discussed a bit of psychological programming that results in our perception of ourselves (self-image) by about age 12. Somewhere along the way, a teacher or parent may have made a comment about their abilities in school. "Tom is really good in English and History but not so good in Math." A statement like that, from an authority figure tends to brand us with a belief. Whenever Tom gets a bad grade in math, he chalks it up to "I'm just not very good with numbers."

Perhaps what should have been said in those earlier days is "Tom does really well in English and History, but he is not devoting enough time to Math. He can easily do the work but he hasn't focused his attention on Math."

What my consultant friend was suggesting was not uncovering your in-born brilliance or gifts in a subject but acquiring competence.

What it takes to develop competence is practice, coaching (perhaps), and a strong desire to do well in the subject.

Why is it we can speak the language of our family? The answer…? We really want to eat and be picked up, and go outside, and get a new bike. We are motivated. We have a strong desire. We practice. We get coaching, (At first from our parents, then teachers).

Accept the idea learning to dribble a basketball or tie your shoes is very similar to learning calculus, trigonometry, plumbing or any other subject. We must want to learn it. We must practice. And we must get coaching if needed.

## Developing Solutions

Jackson's advice was to ensure your solution is good for the short term and in the long term. If you solve the situation in a certain way, will it set a good or bad precedent with your employees, or your clients?

Another consideration is how the solution will fit into the system that already exists.

## Bifocal and Trifocal vision

Imagine a problem inside your corporation has been exposed. A solution that answers the requirement is created. *That solution might be considered transactional in nature.* It solves the problem that has been identified but it may create other problems in the long term, as part of a ripple effect. How do you mitigate this?

One consideration is to look at a problem, not just with a current focus but, through bifocal or even trifocal lenses.

Several years ago, a report on insurance policies and disingenuous sales practices hit the newspapers with a strong negative impact. One mutual company developed a rapid response to ensure agents were aware of the rules. The corporate leaders informed the agents of the new regulations governing insurance illustrations—those long printouts with columns of numbers indicating death benefits and future values.

Immediately, the home office required every local manager to convene a meeting with the agents for whom this manager was responsible, to discuss the changes. An information packet was developed at corporate headquarters to guide the manager's conversation. 100% attendance was required and records would be inspected. (Never make a requirement you aren't prepared to check.)

At the next quarterly training meeting, a higher quality, more polished presentation was provided to all the agents, by a senior executive from the home office with assistance from a home office legal staff member.

The new agent training program underwent immediate scrutiny and adjustment, to ensure the training included the new regulations and no contradictory information appeared in other training modules.

The training department had wisely investigated the problem to develop an immediate or short-term solution. The department and senior management developed a more robust, high-quality program for the midterm solution. In changing the new agent training modules, the corporation had developed a long-range solution. My friend would say they were bringing the issue into focus, not just with glasses, but with bifocal and trifocal lenses.

## Transactional; Integrated, Supplementary and Complementary; and Foundational solutions

Another way to consider solutions is to name the initial fix, the transactional solution. It solves your immediate problem. A customer might not ask for anything other than the transactional solution.

The solution may not fit in their traditional system, but it solves a current issue. A solution that also fits within the normal training delivery system would be seen as your integrated, supplementary and complementary solution. The long-term solution is the foundational change you would need to make in your system and your organization, to eliminate the need for continuing the transactional solution used in taking care of a current shortfall.

Imagine an automobile company has introduced a new gadget for their cars. The company turns to their training department and directs them to come up with an immediate training solution for all the mechanics at the dealerships, and assembly lines. The training department solves the problem with a video explaining the new gadget and how to install, repair, or replace it. Every assembly line employee and mechanic, employed by dealerships, from novice to master must watch this video. This would be a transactional solution.

However, as a solution provider to customers, the team should determine how advanced maintenance and repair information is normally provided to the customer (the mechanics) and how the certification is annotated in their training records.

Are the mechanics primarily taught advanced skills by local front-line supervisors through a mentor system? Is the most natural way to convey the information to novice mechanics through these master mechanics? If so, then your midrange solution might include a train-the-trainer course ensuring your front-line supervisors get firsthand information in greater depth so they are fully prepared to pass on the information to their charges.

Is there a training and certification system that is being neglected in the transactional solution you would want to include? Instead of transactional, these attributes would build the *integrated, supplementary, and complementary* solutions to the issue.

Ultimately, the training department should decide when is the optimum time and where is the best place to provide the basic, or related, information to the new hire? Should it be in the basic mechanic's course you run in-house? Even before you farm them out to the master mechanic who will complete their training, you introduce them to the new gadget. This would be a *foundational* solution to your program.

Consider this situation from the new mechanic's perspective. He or she gets 99% of the advanced, on-the-job, education and training regarding a part or a system from a master mechanic. But, when the novice mechanic asks the master mechanic about this new gadget, the novice is shuffled over to a video with the instruction, "Watch this." Delivering training through videos might not be the normal training delivery method.

After watching the video, the novice asks a specific question, about information not covered in the video. The master mechanic may be stumped for an answer. The master mechanic has received only the training in this video.

A situation like this doesn't build confidence in the novice about the competence of the master mechanic. Again, this is probably not the routine for developing in-depth expertise in the master mechanic.

There is dissonance in the training program, and possibly in record keeping with regard to this one gadget.

What is the most effective way of delivering the training within the organization's established structures?

When you fixate on transactional solutions, never working toward foundational solutions, while neglecting the integrated, supplementary, complementary aspects of your solutions, the transactional solution always seems out of sync and not aligned with normal systems.

You want your solutions to have connectivity with your organization's DNA. You don't want to insert an antigen into your organization that serves as a focus for antibodies. Build and embed your solutions into your current and common processes.

*Forrest Wayne Heard*

# Epilogue

Congratulations on completing this book. I hope you have enjoyed the journey and you have found at least one idea, or technique that has merit. As I advised at the beginning, the methods I intended to discuss were not the result of research or an untried philosophy of management. These were observations of highly effective leaders plying the trade.

Of course, merely reading the words contained in this book won't help one become a better manager or senior executive unless you put some of these ideas into practice. At the beginning, I suggested writing in the margins, keeping a record of what you consider possible ideas for organizational improvement, your skill set in managing, or your effectiveness in reporting to the senior executive.

Now, I suggest you take one of the topics and decide how you could employ the ideas in your organization. Can you begin to be more inclusive in your initial brainstorming sessions that provide ideas and activities for your project? Perhaps you can bring together a team to discuss professional development topics and an implementation plan.

Remember this: During every 12 months, Jackson's leadership team (officers and sergeants) participated in:

- 52 training sessions on the equipment the unit employed, along with the by-the-numbers maintenance of each item

- 24 professional development sessions focused on the knowledge, skills, and abilities necessary for success in their current positions, plus information required to succeed at the next level of leadership

- approximately 12 model unit training events that focused on team skills or new equipment.

Can you imagine the increase in your organization's ability to execute after one year of a similar program, and the increase in skills after several years of applying this level of attention on improving your individuals and your teams? Jackson's program was in addition to the corporate education and training programs.

And in a corporate setting, the mutual insurance company that dominated the Million Dollar Round Table for years, systematically pulled their agents 'off the streets' to sharpen the saws (as Stephen Covey or Benjamin Franklin might suggest).

If you aren't the senior executive, you'll certainly want to discuss the manner in which you deliver the project status report. Is the POA&M sufficient for him, or her? Perhaps, your senior executive wants the greater detail provided at every status report meeting. Will your senior executive accept the role of Project Owner? Even if your senior executive is not on board, you can still employ the POA&M at your level for managing multiple projects for which you are responsible.

One of the hardest team skills to learn but, arguably, the one with the biggest payoff, is increasing your team's capabilities to conduct a structured task analysis for a vision, an idea, or a project. This will take an investment of time in educating the team initially; followed by a talk through, crawl through, walk through, and run through. If you aren't already using a structure to develop your plans, you might need help with this one.

If there is an issue or a vision that you sorely want to influence, and you are the senior executive or you are in a position to be a change agent, I cannot express in strong enough words the effectiveness of getting out of the office to observe, ask questions, and include "Tell me about your ..." to change an organization. When you are asking questions about the issues you want to influence, your subordinate managers and executives will begin to become interested. If they aren't on board, it will be apparent as you visit their operations and production lines. You will have discovered a member of your band of inhibitors.

Perhaps you are completing, or you are somewhere along in the life of, a project and you want to ensure your team learns from the process. This might be an ideal opportunity for you to meet with the key members and discuss how you might go about developing a lessons-learned segment to your project. This resulting 'beware-and-behold' document could form the basis for a class in your professional development program.

If your responsibilities include vehicles or production equipment, and you don't already have a system for bringing your personnel, supervisors, managers, and rising stars up to speed on taking care of the equipment, trouble-shooting it, and taking immediate action when there is an emergency, this might be your start point for putting these ideas into practice.

Wherever you start, and whatever ideas found merit with you, I wish you much success. I will leave you with one final thought about philosophy and success.

It was not uncommon, in the years before the Soviet Union imploded, to hear a teacher or professor espouse from the lectern a comment such as this. "Socialism (or communism) is good in theory; it just hasn't worked in practice." It seems that the system is attracting followers again.

I remember my brother coming home from college and discussing this idea with my father. My father thought for a moment and asked him to consider this: Imagine that someone suggests a design for a bridge. But, every time a bridge using that design was constructed, it collapsed with the first bit of traffic. Would you say that the design was good in theory but didn't work in practice or would you ultimately come to the conclusion that the design is faulty? My dad's conclusion was, if something (philosophy or economic system), doesn't work in practice, it's probably not a good theory.

Or, as John W. Gardner says, "**An excellent plumber is infinitely more admirable than an incompetent philosopher. The society which scorns excellence in plumbing because plumbing is a humble activity, and tolerates shoddiness in philosophy because it is an exalted activity, will have neither good plumbing nor good philosophy. Neither its pipes nor its theories will hold water.**"

In conclusion, as I have said often, this work is not theory but the result of my observations of talented, and very effective leaders who knew how to execute, with excellence. These ideas work in practice.

Good luck as you employ these ideas in your lives and work.

*Forrest Wayne Heard*

# Bibliography

Bossidy, L., & Charan, R. (2002). *EXECUTION; THE DISCIPLINE OF GETTING THINGS DONE.* New York, NY, USA: Crown Business, a Member of Crown Publishing Group, a division of Random House, Inc.

Bossidy, L., & Charan, R. (2004). *CONFRONTING REALITY; Doing What Matters to Get Things Right.* New York, NY, USA: Crown Business, Member of the Crown Publishing Group, a division of Random House, Inc.

Churchill, W. S. (2012). THE POWER OF WORDS; HIS REMARKABLE LIFE RECOUNTED THROUGH HIS WRITINGS AND SPEECHES. (M. Gilbert, Ed.) Boston, MA, USA: Da Capo Press.

Collins, J. (2001). *GOOD TO GREAT; Why Some Companies Make the Leap...and Others Don't.* New York, NY, USA: HarperCollins Publishers, Inc.

Drucker, P. F. (1985, July). Managing People: How to Make People Decisions. *Harvard Business Review.*

Drucker, P. F. (2001). THE ESSENTIAL DRUCKER; The Best of Sixty Years of Peter Drucker's Essential Writings on Management. New York, NY, USA: HarperCollins Publishers, Inc.

Drucker, P. F. (2008). *Management* (Revised ed.). New York: HarperCollins Publishers.

Gerstner, L. V. (2002). *Who Says Elephants Can't Dance? Inside IBM's Historic Turnaround.* Waterville: Thorndike Press; by arrangement with HarperCollins Publishers, Inc.

Goldratt, E. M. (1997). *CRITICAL CHAIN; A Business Novel.* Great Barrington, MA, USA: The North River Press Publishing Corporation.

Goldratt, E. M. (2004). *THE GOAL; A PROCESS OF ONGOING IMPROVEMENT* (Third Revised Edition ed.). Great Barrington, MA, USA: The North River Press Publishing Corporation.

Peters, T., & Austin, N. (1985). *A Passion for Excellence.* New York: Ran House, Inc.

Roberto, P. M. (2009). The Art of Critical Decision Making. *The Great Courses.* Chantilly, VA, USA: The Teaching Company.

Senior, D., & Collins, J. J. (Eds.). (2006). *The Catholic Study Bible, NEW AMERICAN BIBLE* (Second ed.). New York: Oxford University Press.

Walton, M. (1986). *The DEMING Management Method.* New York, NY, USA: The Berkley Publishing Group.

# Glossary

One of my early contributors suggested I provide a glossary to ensure understanding of some of the Army jargon I pepper through this book.

The explanations with these terms are very general in nature to provide a broad understanding to the reader and do not indicate the exact definitions one would see in a military document.

- **Unit**: an organization that can be of any size and structure, (May be called an element).

- **Fire Team**: 5 personnel; led by a Sergeant

- **Squad**: 11 personnel; 2 fire teams; led by a Staff Sergeant

- **Platoon**: 40 personnel: 3 Squads and a Headquarters element (with radios and machine guns); led by a lieutenant (LT). A platoon sergeant (PSG) serves as the senior enlisted advisor to the LT.

- **Company**: 150 personnel: 3 Rifle Platoons; a Headquarters element; and a Mortar Platoon (of approximately 20 personnel); led by a Captain (CPT). A first sergeant (1SG) serves as the senior enlisted advisor to the CPT.

- **Battalion**: 600 personnel: 3 Rifle Companies; a Headquarters Company; a Combat Support Company (with scouts, mortars, and anti-tank platoons); led by a lieutenant colonel (LTC). A command sergeant major (CSM) serves as the senior enlisted advisor to the LTC.

- **Brigade**: 2000 to 4000 personnel: 3 or more Battalions; a Headquarters Company; and various supporting organizations; led by a colonel (COL). A CSM serves as the senior enlisted advisor to the COL.

- **Division**: 15,000 to 20,000 personnel: 3 Brigades; Headquarters Company; supporting battalions; led by a major general (MG). A CSM serves as the senior enlisted advisor. Two other general officers - brigadier generals (BG) - serve as

Assistant Division Commanders. Their portfolios are often organized by maneuver and support.

## Additional organizational elements:

- **Crew**: mortars, machine guns, and anti-tank weapons are considered crew-served weapons with crew members, with different responsibilities, performing specific duties with regard to the weapon.

- **Section**: Two or more squads, or weapons.

- **Special Forces A Team**: Also called an **ODA** - Operational Detachment Alpha, SF Team; **SF Detachment**; 12 personnel; led by a captain. A chief warrant officer (CWO) serves as the executive officer. A master sergeant (MSG) serves as the senior enlisted advisor.

## Weapons:

- **Sight picture** is the term used to describe the alignment of the front and rear sights, with relation to the target.

- **Shot group** is the term used to describe the arrangement of holes in a target made by the bullets fired by one shooter. The closer they are together, the "tighter" the shot group. A tight shot group indicates the shooter is applying the shooting principles well, but the weapon's sight may need to be adjusted. If one adjusts the sights before the shot group is tight, the shots will continue to be all over the target without any improvement in the shooting skills.

- **Misfire** is the term applied to a round that does not fire. If you pull the trigger of a rifle and the round doesn't fire, or you drop a mortar round down the tube and it doesn't fire, you have experienced a misfire.

- **Immediate Action** (rifle) or **Misfire Procedures** (mortar) are the terms applied to taking corrective action when a round doesn't fire.

- The **M16** (now the **M4**) is the basic rifle carried by US Army forces. Designed and built to fire well aimed bullets (rounds) one at a time.

- The **squad automatic weapon (SAW)** is designed to fire multiple rounds with each squeeze of the trigger. There are two SAW gunners in each squad.

- The **machine gun** is made to fire large numbers of rounds at a target, for an extended time. The barrel can be changed quickly to prevent overheating. It is crew-served and can be fired from a bipod or tripod. This weapon significantly increases the firepower of the platoon. Rifle platoons employ two machine guns.

- The **grenade launcher** is a weapon that provides the infantryman with the capability to lob a 40mm 'grenade' several hundred meters. The launch tube is mounted under the rifle (M16/M4) barrel.

- The **mortar** is an indirect fire weapon. The mortar fires a round (60mm, 81mm, or the 4.2inch - also known as a 102mm) very high in the air. After the round reaches apogee, it makes an almost vertical drop. The mortar is assigned to infantry units.

- **Cannons** fire rounds in a lower trajectory (arc) than the mortar, but at much longer ranges, with more powerful warheads. Artillery is the general purpose name for cannons and other large indirect fire weapons. Artillery does not belong to the infantry but is employed in support of the infantry, and other organizations on the battlefield. One of Meloy's canons was **"Always take your mortars with you because you request artillery but you command mortars."** (Canons are statements of faith or rules of conduct, not to be confused with cannons.)

- Depending on the arrangement of the enemy defensive positions, and the terrain, either the mortar or the cannon might be the most effective weapon.

- Grenade launchers, mortars, and artillery have several types of warheads depending on the effect you desire - smoke, high explosive, illumination, etc.

### Close Air Support:

- When the USAF is dropping bombs and firing bullets (strafing) in support of the ground forces that are in a fight with the enemy, it is called close air support (CAS).

### Miscellaneous Terms

**Arms Room**: The secured (locked) room where the weapons are locked and stored when not in use.

**Commissary**: A grocery store located on an Army base.

**DOTMLPF - P**: The mnemonic device used to describe the areas of evaluation when fielding a new piece of equipment, developing a new organization, etc.

**FITCAL**: A mnemonic for inspecting a vehicle and making minor adjustments. Feel, Inspect, Tighten, Clean, Adjust, Lubricate.

**FM Field Manual**: This is a document published by the Army to describe how to conduct a tactical mission (river crossing, ambush, etc.) or employ a weapon.

**JP Joint Publication**: This is a document published by the joint community (Army, Air Force, Navy, and Marines) to describe how joint forces (air, ground, special operations forces, and maritime) are employed or joint missions are conducted.

**MDMP:** Military **Decision - Making Process**: The 7 step process that guides decision making and plan development. It begins with the METT - TC analysis and ends with the production of an order.

**Mess Kit Laundry:** Stations at which metal mess kits and canteens are immersed in boiling water before the Soldier is served food in the field and then washed and sanitized again, after the Soldier has finished his or her meal.

**METT - TC**: A mnemonic for identifying the topics that should be researched during a mission analysis.

**Motor Pool**: An area where the unit's vehicles are parked and maintained when not being used.

**Officer Candidate School:** A commissioning program designed to identify, educate, and train selected enlisted personnel to serve as second lieutenants in the military.

**PACE: Primary, Alternate, Contingency, Emergency**. PACE is the mnemonic to remind planners to have four plans, four ways to communicate, etc.

**PLL: Prescribed Load List:** The basic load of parts that should be stocked for maintaining and repairing any piece of equipment (weapon, communications, vehicle, etc.)

**PMCS: Preventive Maintenance Checks and Services**. PMCS is the protocol for conducting checks, services, and maintenance for a piece of equipment before, during, and after use. PMCS for each piece of equipment is described in the technical manual for that item.

**PX: Post Exchange**. A store located on an Army base.

**ROTC**: One of the programs designed to prepare second lieutenants for service in the military, conducted on campus of universities. The other two commissioning programs are the military academies and officer candidate courses.

**Sets, Kits, and Outfits:** End items, or large pieces of equipment, are generally issued with ancillary equipment. The full issue of end items and additional parts fall under the umbrella category of sets, kits, and outfits. A field oven may come with pots, potholders, pans, and spatulas.

**SOP: Standing Operating Procedure**: Often called Standard Operating Procedure. SOPs describe how a unit performs a particular mission, or activity.

**USR and DRRS: Unit Status Report and Defense Readiness Reporting System**. USR was the term for readiness reporting. The current terminology is DRRS, a robust database in which unit commanders report the unit's readiness to perform its mission.

**TM: Technical Manual**: This is a document published by the Army to explain how to inspect, and maintain a piece of equipment, be it weapon, communications, vehicle, etc.

*Forrest Wayne Heard*

# Quotations

Some of the quotations offered in the book and in this section were spoken time and again, but not always word for word. The author offers a couple of variations for some quotations here.

| Chapter | Page | Author | Quote |
|---|---|---|---|
| Opening Leaf | 2 | **Drucker** | "A manager sets objectives- A manager organizes – A manager motivates and communicates – A manager, by establishing yardsticks, measures – A manager develops people." |
| Opening Leaf | 2 | **Drucker** | "Traditionally, we have searched for the miracle worker with the magic wand to turn an ailing organization around. To establish, maintain, and restore a theory, however, does not require a Genghis Khan or a Leonardo da Vinci in the executive suite. What is required is not genius; it is hard work. It is not being clever; it is being conscientious. It is what CEOs are paid for." |
| Preface | 19 | **Jackson** | "The After-Action Report starts now!" He also stressed the After-Action Review begins now. |
| Preface | 19 | **Ford** | "It is always possible to do a thing better the second time." |
| Preface | 19 | **Aristotle** | "We are what we repeatedly do. Excellence, then, is not an act, but a habit." (From the Will Durant translation) |
| Preface | 20 | **Tree Farmer** | "Even a hole has to be managed." |
| Preface | 20 | **Atlanta business consultant** | "Not all Soldiers are like Uriah." |
| Preface | 21 | **Rohn** | "What is easy to do is easy NOT to do." |
| Preface | 24 | **adage** | "When the student is ready, the teacher will appear." |
| Preface | 24 | **Collins** | "As Peter Drucker shows right here, in these pages, the very best leaders are first and foremost effective managers. Those who seek to lead but fail to manage |

| Chapter | Page | Author | Quote |
|---|---|---|---|
|  |  |  | will become either irrelevant or dangerous, not only to their organizations, but to society." |
| Preface | 24 | **Deming** | "To manage one must lead. To lead, one must understand the work that he and his people are responsible for." |
| Preface | 25 | **A Definition** | The actions you take, and the environment you create for those with whom you work, to accomplish worthwhile goals and objectives with your family, community, work, nation, and the world. |
| Preface | 25 | **Drucker** | "Productivity is not the responsibility of the worker, but of the manager." |
| Preface | 28 | **Deming** | "If you can't describe your process, you don't have one." |
| Preface | 28 | **Carnegie** | "People support a world they helped create." |
| Preface | 29 | **Drucker** | "Plans are only good intentions unless they immediately degenerate into hard work." "A decision is a commitment to action." |
| Preface | 29 | **Drucker** | "No decision has, in fact, been made until carrying it out has become somebody's work assignment and responsibility--and with a deadline. Until then, it's still only a hope." |
| Preface | 30 | **Collins** | "A culture of <u>discipline</u> is not a principle of business, it is a principle of greatness." "Greatness is not a function of circumstance. Greatness, it turns out, is largely a matter of conscious choice, and <u>discipline</u>." |
| Preface | 33 | **Jackson** | "Maintenance is a command responsibility." |
| Preface | 33 | **Jackson** | "The training isn't over until the equipment is ready to go to war again." Or "The deployment isn't over until the equipment is read to go to war again." |
| Preface | 34 | **Gerstner** | "(…) you cannot run a successful enterprise from behind a desk." |
| Preface | 34 | **Drucker** | "Effective decision makers know this and follow a rule, which the military developed long ago. The commander who makes a decision does not rely on reports to see how it is being carried out. Instead, the commander goes out and looks for himself or herself." |

| Chapter | Page | Author | Quote |
|---|---|---|---|
| | | | "Not that he distrusts the subordinate; he has learned from experience to distrust communications." |
| Preface | 35 | LTG Hooper | "After serving as a lieutenant under Jackson, everything else came easy". |
| Preface | 36 | Deming | "Managing by results-like looking in the rear view mirror." |
| Preface | 38 | Atlanta Business Consultant | If you have a problem, develop a process. |
| Preface | 38 | Atlanta Business consultant | "If You Can Tie Your Shoes, You Can Learn Physics". |
| 1 | 43 | Deming | "If you can't explain your process, you don't have one." |
| 1 | 43 | Einstein | "If you can't explain it simply, you don't understand it well enough." |
| 1 | 43 | adage | "What got you there, won't keep you there." Marshall Goldsmith wrote a book, "What Got You Here Won't Get You There." |
| 1 | 45 | Drucker | "Plans are only good intentions unless they immediately degenerate into hard work." |
| 1 | 48 | Jackson | "The After-Action Review starts now." |
| 2 | 49 | Adage | Prescription without diagnosis is malpractice. |
| 2 | 50 | Ohmae | "Analysis is the critical starting point of strategic thinking." |
| 2 | 50 | Voltaire: | No problem can withstand the assault of sustained thinking. |
| 2 | 50 | Unknown | Never use inside jargon on outside audiences |
| 2 | 53 | Special Forces Warrant Officer | Like high school math, it helps to show your work. |
| 2 | 60 | Deming: | "We should work on our process, not the outcome of our processes." |
| 2 | 61 | Special Forces Warrant Officer | Find out where 'Murphy' lives. |

| Chapter | Page | Author | Quote |
|---------|------|--------|-------|
| 2 | 61 | **Heard** | …always endorsed, but rarely enforced. |
| 2 | 61 | **Deming** | "If you don't not know how to ask the right question, you discover nothing." |
| 2 | 61 | **Heard** | "Don't eat the bananas." |
| 2 | 62 | **Deming** | "If you can't describe what you are doing as a process, you don't know what you're doing." |
| 2 | 63 | **Katz** | inclusive brainstorming. |
| 2 | 65 | **Archilochus** | "We don't rise to the level of our expectations, we fall to the level of our training." |
| 2 | 66 | **Goethe** | Everything is hard, before it is easy. |
| 2 | 69 | **Aristotle** | "For the things we have to learn before we can do them, we learn by doing them." |
| 2 | 70 | **Von Moltke** | "No plan of operations extends with any certainty beyond the first contact with the main hostile force." This quotation is often summarized as 'no plan survives first contact with the enemy'. |
| 2 | 70 | **Kroesen** | "If you are developing plans for combat and they don't include what to do when you are getting shot at, it's not much of a plan." |
| 3 | 71 | **Jackson** | "Fix the problem, not the blame." |
| 3 | 71 | **Heard** | …the background and the backbone… |
| 3 | 72 | **Jackson** | "You either manage the calendar or it manages you." |
| 3 | 72 | **Deming** | "You manage the cause, not the effect." |
| 3 | 75 | **Jackson** | "The After-Action Report starts now!" |
| 3 | 75 | **Jackson** | "A short pencil is better than a long memory." |
| 3 | 75 | **Jackson** | "A dull pencil is better than a sharp memory." |
| 3 | 76 | **Rohn** | "The box is small. I can only fit a yes or a no. If it's a yes, no discussion is necessary and if it's a no, I understand the reason for that answer too." |
| 3 | 78 | **Effective Sergeant** | "I put them on my schedule". |
| 3 | 82 | **Special Forces Warrant Officer** | "No one pays to watch a clown juggle just one ball". |
| 3 | 84 | **GEN Tackaberry** | "If a leader spends more than two hours a day behind his desk, he's just plain lazy." |

| Chapter | Page | Author | Quote |
|---|---|---|---|
| 3 | 84 | **Gerstner** | "I have always believed you cannot run a successful enterprise from behind a desk." |
| 3 | 87 | **Tree Farmer** | "Even a hole has to be managed." |
| 3 | 88 | **Stang** | Have you talked to the troops today? Don't forget the wrench turners, and spoons. Remember, the only thing you lead from behind this desk, is a pencil. |
| 4 | 91 | **Deming** | "Learning is not compulsory…neither is survival." |
| 4 | 92 | **Deming** | "The aim of leadership is not merely to find and record failures of men, but to remove the causes of failure; to help people to do a better job with less effort." |
| 4 | 93 | **Jackson** | "The training is not over until the equipment is ready to go to war again." |
| 4 | 97 | **Jackson** | "Fix the problem, not the blame." |
| 4 | 97 | **Deming** | "A bad system will beat a good person every time." |
| 4 | 98 | **Jackson** | "Is anyone bleeding?" "Are there any units in a firefight and running low on ammunition?" "Those are the only two situations we consider emergencies. Everything else is just doing business." |
| 4 | 98 | Submariner | "All the solutions are down here." |
| 5 | 103 | **Atlanta business consultant** | "You hire qualified applicants, but you train good employees." |
| 5 | 103 | **Atlanta business consultant** | "What if I train them and they leave?" A better question to ask may be "What if you don't train them, and they stay?" |
| 5 | 104 | **Collins** | … get the right people on the bus and in the right seats, and the wrong people off the bus. |
| 5 | 106 | **Drucker** | We now accept the fact that learning is a lifelong process of keeping abreast of change. And the most pressing task is to teach people how to learn. |
| 5 | 106 | **Special Forces Warrant Officer** | "Audibles are always allowed, but we have to know how to line up at the scrimmage." |
| 5 | 108 | **Roberto** | "How we learn is what we learn." |
| 5 | 111 | **Jackson** | "Hope is not a means." |

| Chapter | Page | Author | Quote |
|---------|------|--------|-------|
| 5 | 116 | **Ahrendt** | "I believe succession planning is one of the greatest responsibilities you have as a leader – so when your time comes to move on, your team not only doesn't miss a beat but gains in momentum, embracing new challenges and realizing future opportunities. |
| 6 | 119 | **Jackson** | "…the exercise isn't over, until the equipment is ready to go to war again." |
| 6 | 124 | **Gerstner** | "I have always believed you cannot run a successful enterprise from behind a desk." |
| 6 | 126 | **Galatians 6:9** | Let us not grow tired of doing good, for in due time we shall reap our harvest, if we do not give up. |
| 6 | 126 | **Churchill** | "If you have an important point to make, don't try to be subtle or clever. Use a pile driver. Hit the point once. Then come back and hit it again. Then hit it a third time – a tremendous whack." |
| 6 | 126 | **Heard** | …always endorsed, rarely enforced. |
| 6 | 128 | **Special Forces Warrant Officer** | When one is detected, many are suspected. |
| 6 | 128 | **Gerstner** | "All of this takes enormous commitment from the CEO to communicate, communicate, and communicate some more." |
| 6 | 132 | **Adage** | Soldiers REspect the leader who INspects what he EXpects. |
| 6 | 132 | **Adage** | If you expressed your INtention, you must give the initiative your ATtention. |
| 6 | 132 | **Gerstner** | People don't do what you expect but what you inspect. |
| 7 | 135 | **Lord Vader** | "…Commander. I'm here to put you back on schedule." |
| 7 | 135 | **Boatswain** | …"left side back paddle; give way together". |
| 7 | 137 | **Latin saying** | "De minimis non curat praetor" |
| 7 | 139 | **Meloy** | "Tell me about your …….." |
| 7 | 142 | **Meloy** | "In combat, you request air support and you request artillery. You command mortars." |
| 7 | 142 | **Churchill** | …he was "loosely educated" |
| 7 | 145 | **Jackson** | Mortars are the only indirect fire assets we command. They are the most responsive indirect |

| Chapter | Page | Author | Quote |
|---|---|---|---|
| | | | asset and must be used routinely. Mortar crews must be 100% filled with qualified personnel and backup personnel must be trained. Leaders must ensure that squads and platoons perform to standard. Routinely, the Battalion will administer a Mortar Safety Officer / NCO Course to certify Indirect Fire Safety Officer and NCOs. |
| 7 | 145 | **Patton** | "There is only one sort of discipline - PERFECT DISCIPLINE. Men cannot have good battle discipline and poor administrative discipline. |
| 7 | 149 | **Rickover** | "A good manager must have unshakeable determination and tenacity. Deciding what needs to be done is easy, getting it done is more difficult. Good ideas are not adopted automatically. They must be driven into practice with courageous impatience. Once implemented they can be easily overturned or subverted through apathy or lack of follow-up, so a continuous effort is required. Too often, important problems are recognized but no one is willing to sustain the effort needed to solve them." |
| 7 | 151 | **Deming** | "If you don't know how to ask questions, you discover nothing." |
| 8 | 154 | **Adage** | "What got you there, won't keep you there" |
| 8 | 156 | **Special Forces Warrant Officer** | "Do you want my sympathy, or advice." |
| 8 | 158 | **General Officer** | "Sometimes you have to slow down, to speed up." |
| 8 | 158 | **Atlanta Business Consultant** | "When you delegate, you've got to pay your premiums." Or "You must pay the premiums and keep them up-to-date." |
| 9 | 168 | **Rommel** | "The best form of welfare for the troops is first-rate training." |
| 10 | 171 | **The Captain** | "What we've got here is failure to communicate." |
| 10 | 171 | **Drucker** | "The second thing to do to manage oneself and to become effective is to take responsibility for communications." |
| 10 | 174 | **Jackson** | "Food is part of the Soldier's pay." |

| Chapter | Page | Author | Quote |
|---|---|---|---|
| 10 | 175 | **Tracy** | "It's not only a good idea to think on paper, it also helps to remember on paper." |
| 10 | 177 | **Drucker** | "Not that he distrusts the subordinate; he has learned from experience to distrust communications." |
| 10 | 177 | **Drucker** | "I trust my people. I just don't trust communications; mine to them or theirs to me." |
| 10 | 177 | **Churchill** | A **lie** gets halfway around the world before the **truth** has a chance to get its pants on. |
| 11 | 180 | **Florer** | "We will be successful when..." |
| 12 | 187 | **Adage** | ...key to good writing is not to write so that an idea can be understood, but to write in such a way that the message can't be misunderstood. |
| 12 | 187 | **Broadway tradition** | ...an amateur practices until he can get it right; a professional practices until he can't get it wrong. |
| 12 | 187 | **Deming** | "Build quality into a product throughout production." |
| 12 | 188 | **Dodge** | "You cannot inspect quality into a product." |
| 12 | 188 | **Atlanta Business Consultant** | Have a problem? Develop a process. |
| 12 | 189 | **Drucker** | "If a crisis happens--the first time it happens, one fixes it. But if it happens again, then one finds out the cause and fixes it so that the crisis never happens again." |
| 12 | 190 | **Vader** | "You may dispense with the pleasantries, Commander. I'm here to put you back on schedule." |
| 12 | 192 | **Drucker:** | "No matter how hard managers try to keep their decisions a secret--and some still try very hard--people decisions cannot be hidden. They are imminently visible." |
| 12 | 194 | **Drucker** | "Executives who do not make the effort to get their people decisions right do more than risk poor performance. They risk losing their organization's respect." |

| Chapter | Page | Author | Quote |
|---------|------|--------|-------|
| 12 | 195 | **Drucker** | "If the job is designed for an individual rather than for a task, then it has to be restructured every time there is a change in the incumbent. And, as experienced managers know, one cannot restructure one job. There is a true "domino effect", a true chain reaction. Restructuring a job usually means restructuring a score of jobs, moving people around, and upsetting everybody. And for this reason, jobs have to be designed to fit a task, rather than a particular person." |
| 12 | 195 | **German business saying** | Gut genug? Die Kunde entscheidet. ("Good enough? The customer will decide." |
| 12 | 201 | **Heard** | Why senior leaders should say "Not yet" instead of "No". |
| 12 | 204 | **Rohn** | "There is always plenty of money. It's your philosophy that needs to change." |
| 12 | 205 | **Lockheed Engineer** | "Put a sharp pencil to it." |
| 12 | 208 | **Adage** | "He couldn't train people to pour water out of boot, even if the instructions were written on the bottom of the heel." |
| 12 | 209 | **Tracy** | Think on Paper; Remember on Paper |
| 12 | 210 | **Drucker** | Follow effective action with quiet reflection. From the quiet reflection will come even more effective action. |
| 12 | 214 | **Atlanta Business Consultant** | If you can tie your shoes, you can learn physics. |
| Epilogue | 223 | **Garner** | "An excellent plumber is infinitely more admirable than an incompetent philosopher. The society which scorns excellence in plumbing because plumbing is a humble activity, and tolerates shoddiness in philosophy because it is an exalted activity, will have neither good plumbing nor good philosophy. Neither its pipes nor its theories will hold water." |

*Forrest Wayne Heard*

# Author Bio

**MR. WAYNE HEARD** is a former Green Beret Officer, who is living in Europe and works in support of Department of Defense.

Because of Wayne's reputation in the fields of writing, teaching, training, and project management, while in uniform, he was called out of retirement in 2004 and asked to help develop and shepherd a new program for the Army—Personnel Recovery— formerly known as combat search and rescue operations.

Initially, he helped write the Army's how-to book on the subject and then worked in the Pentagon to help guide the creation of the Army's program. Afterwards, Wayne worked with units in Iraq and Afghanistan in planning, preparing, and responding to events that had the potential to result in captivity situations. Wayne also worked with the Drug Enforcement Administration to prepare their agents working overseas in high risk areas. He has written several magazine articles on leadership and management.

Wayne began his military career in the 82nd Airborne Division in 1972. In 1977, he was commissioned as an Infantry officer through Officer Candidate School, graduating as the Distinguished Leadership Graduate

After completing Ranger school, Lieutenant Heard returned to the 82nd Airborne Division and led rifle and mortar platoons. In 1979, he completed the Special Forces Officers Course and served as a Green Beret Team Leader in 5th Special Forces Group. Wayne also graduated with honors from his Advanced Officers Course.

In July 1990, just two weeks before the Iraqi army invaded Kuwait, Wayne was selected to be the Operations Officer (S3) of 1st Battalion 10th Special Forces Group. Responding to a no-notice alert to prepare the unit for combat search and rescue operations in northern Iraq, he organized and managed the staff and team training. Wayne also served as the Executive Officer (XO) of the battalion during OPERATION DESERT STORM. In ARMY magazine articles and his book, he describes the training program that resulted in comprehensive mission analysis process that became the hallmark for effective combat planning.

In the area of project management, in addition to managing the development and implementation of the Personnel Recovery program for the Army, Wayne helped plan the closing of an Army base in Bad Tölz, Germany and subsequent move of the unit and their families to Stuttgart. He led the staff in preparing and executing the base closure plan even while the unit was participating in combat operations. Immediately after cessation of hostilities, he organized the support to Special Forces teams operating camps containing 200K refugees.

Wayne is the proud father of three sons and a daughter.